INTENTIONAL PARENTING

DR YVONNE SUM

Dear Claire,

Here's to parenting as a leadership development metaphor... let me know how you enjoy learning from your 'kids'!

Doubleday

love,
Yvonne
xx

Dedicated to my (un)intentional role models who inspired this book: Jerry and Alice, Jett and Xian.

A Doubleday book
Published by Random House Australia Pty Ltd
Level 3, 100 Pacific Highway, North Sydney NSW 2060
www.randomhouse.com.au

First published by Doubleday in 2013

Addresses for companies within the Random House Group can be found at www.randomhouse.com.au/offices.

National Library of Australia
Cataloguing-in-Publication Entry

Sum, Yvonne.
Intentional parenting: how to get results for both you and your kids / Yvonne Sum.

ISBN 978 1 74275 358 4 (pbk.)

Parenting.
Child rearing.
Families.

649.1

Cover design by Christabella Designs
Internal design and typesetting by Post Pre-Press Group
Printed in Australia by Griffin Press, an accredited ISO AS/NZS 14001:2004 Environmental Management System printer

Random House Australia uses papers that are natural, renewable and recyclable products and made from wood grown in sustainable forests. The logging and manufacturing processes are expected to conform to the environmental regulations of the country of origin.

Contents

Foreword
by Jan Roberts

Congratulations, Yvonne, on bringing 'The Seven Rs of Parenting' to the world!

As someone who has been a passionate parent herself, while promoting more enlightened parenting practices for almost thirty years, I'm delighted to see all of the things that are integral to healthier, happier families so eloquently presented in *Intentional Parenting*.

What I like best about the book is Yvonne's ability to give her words a human face. *Intentional Parenting* is not some theoretical treatise, but a wise compilation of enlightened parenting practices that she has carefully considered then tried and tested with positive results. She's done it herself and you, the reader, can share in her wisdom – as well as the doubts and occasional uncertain steps. At the same time, you'll be able to feel the positive achievements of the whole family.

How many parents embark on the most important career of their lives with less preparation than they commit to their wedding day? How many couples step into parenting with only a fraction of the knowledge that they bring to their professions?

Today, when having a family is too often seen as the next 'achievement', after education, career, home, travel and security are all in place, it is important that parents have access to tools that encourage a more holistic view of parenting. Being a parent should be enormously satisfying and richly rewarding. However, in our modern society, many parents feel more challenged by their roles than rewarded. While most parenting training is 'on the job', *Intentional Parenting* supports this amazing journey of being a truly effective and fully connected parent.

From our first introduction as potential collaborators, I was inspired by Yvonne's ability to communicate her message. As we got to know one another, it became clear that our passion for parenting had taken each of us and our respective families down similar roads, even though more than two decades separated those parenting experiences.

But more importantly, we both believe in the importance of the family. We believe families of whatever size or persuasion are our future, and that our society has no more urgent task than to foster their physical, mental and emotional health.

In reading *Intentional Parenting*, I hope that many

parents will be inspired to embrace their roles with more passion and compassion, and as a consequence will be more completely fulfilled by their parenting roles!

Jan Roberts, bestselling author of the Better Babies series
Sydney, Australia

www.buildingbetterbabies.com
www.betterbabies.well4life.com.au

Introduction

Everyone belongs to a tribe. It is not just the football club or the mothers' group. In a world powered by the instant accessibility of the internet, there are many different tribes catering for every aspect of your life. Navigating these tribes is a tricky business. It takes leadership.

The first tribe we learn from is our family. At an early age I learned how to be sociable from my mother and how to be a ruthless and unsentimental de-clutterer from my father. I just accepted those traits as natural. What I had not expected when my children – Jett and Xian – came along was how they would absorb my traits and reflect them straight back at me. Just like my dad, I had become quite the tidiness freak – everything had its place. For example, the three-tiered basket in the laundry became a sorting of 'whites', 'coloured' and 'darks', and God forbid the tribal member who mixed the darks with the whites. I did not realise how overbearing and controlling I was until Jett started to mirror me. He began demanding there be more order in the household and reprimanding his little sister for not putting things back where they belonged. Oops! Cruel was my awareness: 'Mirror, Mirror in the home. Who is the monster that set this tone?'

I had been successful in business and a good leader in the workplace. Once I became a full-time mother I realised that I could not just let the development of my children evolve in a chaotic fashion. This tribe needed leadership – and I was the one to provide it.

As soon as I decided to become an 'intentional parent' – actively, purposefully involving myself in my children's journey through life – everything changed. There were lessons everywhere. I drew on my successful years as a leader in the corporate world and applied what I had learned there to my family. It sounds like I became a dictator – but, remember, I was already a control freak. If anything, becoming an intentional parent and leader of my tribe made everything more relaxed. And happier.

When I took a good look at leading my family, I identified seven foundation stones of successful parenting: the 'seven Rs of parenting'. Each one is fully explored in this book. Together they are the basis for leading your family tribe. They also teach you the most important rule of successful leadership: humility. This is the ability to show vulnerability and to allow others in the tribe to take strength – and to lead at times too. My seven foundation stones are all equally applicable in business. But, unlike a leader in a giant corporation, or even a small one, you cannot sack your family *and* you have a very high investment in their future success.

While you are encouraging your children to learn and grow, you are learning and growing too. You are not just a leader but a 'playpal' – an acronym for *Practising Leader Avidly Yearning Partnerships At Learning*. Intentional parenting is a journey that begins with your conscious decision to become a leader and a playpal to your family.

Let's begin that journey together.

PART ONE

Why Intentional Parenting?

ONE

Leading from the Heart

Legend has it that a long time ago there lived many gods. Some of the gods decided that humankind deserved to be given a great treasure to help in their evolution. But many of the gods had reservations about this because they felt that humans did not deserve this treasure: 'They are simply not good enough. They are forever fighting among themselves. They don't deserve this magic. They don't deserve this treasure. So we shall hide it from them.' One god said, 'We shall hide it at the top of the Great Mountain – they'll never find it there.' Another suggested, 'We should put it under the rapids of the Great River – they will never find it there.' After much debate, the smallest god piped up, 'Excuse me, I think I have an idea. Let's hide the Great Treasure in all human hearts. They will never find it in there.'

Parenting, like stepping up to become a manager, is a leadership privilege that you may have actively chosen or it may have been bestowed upon you by surprise. Parenting is your commitment to a learning partnership with your child or children, a partnership that not only grows your children but also develops you in the process. It is a general misconception that you as parents (like managers) have to have all the answers. You don't. Some of the greatest resources waiting to be tapped lie in your children and you will find them by asking questions – questions to which you don't have the answers.

The advent of parenting can shake you to the core. My life was going along fine – and then I had children.

When I became pregnant I was wracked with doubt. Who was I to bring up another human being when I was hardly sure of how to look after myself? I could have been a classic case study of antenatal depression. My life as I knew it was truly ended. I was so terrified about my prospective role that I developed pre-eclampsia (high blood pressure) in the third trimester.

A sense of overwhelming unconditional love is said to envelop the mother when a child is born. In the delirium of my labour – or simply hallucinating from my endorphins – as Jett ventured into the world, I imagined him talking to me: 'You were in this playground first,' he said. 'Be my tour guide. I have a destiny you cannot change. Relax and enjoy the ride. Nothing you do – good or bad – will stop me getting there. It can challenge or support me though. Just love me, Mum!'

And that's what I did – and what I continue to do. I understand what this heartfelt message from within means. 'If what I do diverts Jett from where he is destined, he will rebel in order to get back onto his track. If I inspire him as he is learning to become himself, then he has an easier road to his fate. My job is to observe Jett as best I can so I can inspire him on his way.' And so began my learning partnership with my child. My blood pressure dropped to normal immediately.

I also consciously came to the following realisations:

1. I don't have to have all the answers.
2. I don't have to do it exactly as my parents did.
3. I can make this a positive opportunity to grow.

When Jett was born, I opened up my senses to observe him constantly. The fact that I found my own child to be the most gorgeous being made it easy for me to give him 100 per cent of my attention.

It has been said that no book can give a complete guide on how to be a parent. I beg to differ. The book is the child: so read the book that is the child – and the rest comes easily. I realised I did not have to teach Jett everything. What a relief. Instead, Jett taught me more than I could ever imagine. He allowed me to see the beauty in our world through new curious eyes and to marvel at a lot of things I had taken for granted: a new leaf on a tree, a crawling caterpillar, the patterns raindrops make on the car window. I started to appreciate music from the classical composers, which always soothed him into a trance (he has a natural gift for music and plays amazing violin and piano by ear now). By the age of two, his favourites included Mozart's *Marriage of Figaro*, Bach's *Air on the G String* and Saint-Saëns' *Carnival of the Animals*. He was about the same age when I started reading him to sleep with Shakespeare – he especially loved *Romeo and Juliet*. I realised Jett was demonstrating the wisdom and genius that we are all born with but which is gradually eroded by time and society.

Lesson #1: The joy of learning partnerships

My path to becoming a leader involved me learning some important lessons from my children first.

I learned to be imperfectly perfect. I have a partner in my child as I learn about my parenting role. Go with the flow. Learn from one another.

My daughter Xian, who is two years younger than Jett, has taught me plenty as well: the joy of her love of learning, which is always obvious from the broadest of beaming smiles; her ability to read and understand mathematical concepts at age two; her amazing ability to engage people of any age into connecting with her, and the joy of movement and dance. We are currently navigating Antoine de Saint-Exupéry's novella *The Little Prince*, both for its excellent story and its exploration of the human condition.

Xian also taught me about open and honest communications in an unusual way. In the last month of my pregnancy, she breached and my doctor recommended a caesarian. I took a moment to connect with Xian in utero and asked her to collaborate as best she could so that I could have a natural birth. Within the week, she had turned and I delivered her naturally with hardly twenty minutes of labour. Woo hoo! What a great team effort!

One of the best things about not having all the answers is that it makes you more curious about finding them.

Lesson #2: Be curious and explore the world

The next lesson that my children taught me is to see the world from their point of view. In their world, there is no such thing as failure. There is an insatiable need to explore why the grass is green and the sky blue. Curiosity is a great thing to have as a learner. How beautiful it is for parents to retain childlike spontaneity, creativity, exploration and the ability to live life with a sense of wonder! As learning partners navigating our world, our children can bring out this neoteny, or sense of curiosity, and wonder in the parent. The world gets curiouser and curiouser for us again. How magnificent to discover this amazing planet that we live in, again.

It seemed a long time since I had enjoyed the rhythmical pitter-patter of raindrops, or watched patiently as a caterpillar grazed the tender leaves on my favourite shrub, or I deliciously caressed the stippled waxy lemon rind as if fondling a well-loved pet.

Lesson #3: Being present

Jett and Xian taught me patience, to linger over short connected moments of bliss every day, to enjoy seeing the world from their perspective and to ask for help.

Lesson #4: Read the book that is your child

The most important lesson of all: you may learn more about yourself through learning about your children.

TWO

The Essence of Leadership

In years past parents controlled their families. They ensured traditions were followed and they commanded discipline. They made the rules and set routines. Children were preferably seen and not heard. Parents used two levers to control their families: the hope of reward (usually praise and attention) and the fear of their wrath and punishment.

This method of command and control management will not work with today's tribal mentality. Now, parents must lead. For the last decade, as I've worked with parents and leaders in organisations, it has become apparent to me that the leadership that works in today's complex environment has great similarities to the type of leadership found in the ancient past, in families, tribes and the wider community. We have to go further back in order to go forward.

Tribal leadership is a different way of looking at the world. In the context of the tribe, parents need to understand two critical elements:

1. The *essence* of their leadership. This is what informs the actions of tribal leaders. Their personal essence – the overriding philosophy that underpins their decisions and actions – enables authenticity to thrive.
2. The *actions* of their leadership. Essence is nothing without action. Tribal leaders actively work to ensure their own actions encourage and enable their followers to achieve great outcomes and to develop to their full potential.

When these two elements are present, good leadership is possible. And when these two elements are connected by learning partnerships, *great* leadership is possible.

For example, before Jett was born I wanted to be the perfect parent. I looked for books, courses and role models and found there was not just one but a multitude of them. This search for perfection became the *essence* of my leadership as a parent: to strive for the very best. A course on multiplying your baby's intelligence particularly caught my attention and I flew to Philadelphia in the United States to do the program. I found its content powerful and the philosophy of the parent and child sharing the joy of learning together stimulating. But I realised it would only work if I pay attention to my child, which means *being present* with my child.

This translated into *action* when I was asked to present at a women's conference on parenting in Malaysia. In the course of reflecting on what worked in my own parenting journey with my children, I realised that in order to be a better parent I looked to my own role models: my parents and grandparents. That made me ask myself what kind of role model I wanted to be for my children. My parents had always said that parenting was about 'paying forward': don't expect your children to pay you back for what you do for them – instead, encourage them to be the best they can be and one day, hopefully, they will 'pay it forward' to their kids. I realised that to achieve the essence of my leadership – wanting to be a perfect parent so that my children would reach their highest potential – I needed to turn that idea into action and lead the life that is best for me. I did not want my children to become a clone of myself but I would inspire them to be the best they could be for themselves. It meant I had to take the action of being the best I could be. I started to look at trying new things to stretch my comfort zone. Eventually that led me to leave the safe haven of dentistry in order to explore the exciting world of leadership coaching and begin the journey to reach my own highest potential.

There are four key elements to becoming the leader of your family tribe.

Before I list them, let me tell you a story.

When Jett and Xian were four and two years of age they would constantly argue with each other in front of me – but never when their father or grandparents were around. Finally, I had had enough. When they erupted into another tirade of shouting, I stepped in and said loudly, 'Enough! Jett, into your room. Xian, you too. Time out.' They obeyed instantly.

I went into Xian's room. 'Why do you both squabble loudly like a flock of cockatoos when I am around and never with Dad or Nene [Grandma]?' I asked.

'You never seem to mind, Mum,' she said.

'What makes you think I don't mind?'

'Dad and Nene tell us loud and clear when we start getting a bit too noisy,' Xian said. 'So we know they mind, and so we stop.'

Interesting. I wandered into Jett's room and asked the same question. I got a similar reply. Very interesting.

I gathered my two children together, thanked them for their insights and told them that, actually, I did mind when they made a racket. I just did not show it in the manner their father and grandmother did. They both assured me that they did not like me being upset and promised to do better. They asked me to let them know as soon as I was getting upset so that they would learn when they were crossing the line. They hugged me and said they were glad we had had the conversation. I kissed them and promised to give them immediate feedback should it happen again. After a few reminders, my flock of cockatoos disappeared to be replaced by the angels that they are.

That exchange taught me the four key elements to becoming a leader of my little tribe.

Authenticity: leading self and others in context

He who knows others is learned. He who knows himself is wise.

– Lao Tzu

Leadership of any tribe begins with self-awareness in two areas:

1. our values, strengths and vulnerabilities
2. the context in which we lead.

This self-awareness is the steadfast platform by which we can lead our tribe with empathy.

As a parent, I am comfortable to let my children know that I have areas of vulnerability and that I don't always have the answers. For example, when I am stuck on the frustrations of the electronic age, I often call on Jett to help me solve the problems. He has an innate ability to understand these things, which I don't. In allowing him to see my weaknesses he sees the authenticity of our relationship.

Being present: opening up the senses to observe and understand

There are only two ways to live your life. One is as though nothing is a miracle. The other is as though everything is a miracle.

– Albert Einstein

Understanding yourself is critical to effective leadership – and so is the ability to understand others. Leadership is relational and is only effective when leaders get inside the heads and hearts of their followers and understand each team member's unique situation.

Kids are great at staying in the present. They don't get hysterical about the historical: what's past is gone. They don't plan too much either – instead, they stay in the moment. They remind us about what we have forgotten – or not practised.

When both my kids were breast-feeding it was a wonderful privilege being able to spend that time bonding with them in the unhurried nature of this beautiful process. I could not multi-task. I simply had to sit still and be present as my child breastfed. It is such a meditative and connecting way to be.

As the children got older, I remember Jett and Xian watching a spider weave its web slowly. As I sat there with them for what seemed like hours I was totally in the present and was overcome by the magnificence of nature and our world.

Common sense: strategising before acting

All our knowledge begins with the senses, proceeds then to the understanding, and ends with the reason. There is nothing higher than reason.

– Immanuel Kant

Common sense requires leaders to apply a degree of intelligence in relation to the performance of their followers by being insightful, strategic and tactical.

Xian has an ability to get to the bottom of an emotional situation better than I can. So, when we were making a decision about whether I was to take up an overseas assignment and leave my kids and husband at home for a period while I got acclimatised to the new culture, her wise and honest take on this was: 'Mum, I know I can't talk you out of going – and I won't because this is good for you and I wouldn't want to get in the way. So we are coming with you. Why? Because, I need you near me. I am a girl going through puberty and I need my mum as the only other woman in the household to help me through this!'

Inspiration: leading by learning in partnership

Just don't give up trying to do what you really want to do. Where there's love and inspiration, I don't think you can go wrong.

– Ella Fitzgerald

Without inspiration, there is only a fractured vision.

As leaders, we need to know and then show enough of ourselves – including our values, life experiences, strengths and weaknesses – to create a sense of community through embracing a purpose bigger than ourselves while remaining authentic. And we need to celebrate the significance of others while exciting them to exceptional performance, and collaborating with respect.

Parents don't always have to be the ones to define the vision. I have been pleasantly surprised at the source of unexpected inspiration.

Jett was thirteen and it was his first month at high school. The school was holding a two-hour study skills workshop to help parents and children prepare for examinations later in the year. I was proud of the examination techniques I had used in my glory days in the education system and was enthusiastic to attend. But I knew one can never be a prophet in one's home and that it was best that Jett heard it from the experts at school. Not from Mum.

That evening at the workshop I took copious notes that validated my own sound exam preparation methods. As we left the auditorium, Jett eyed my notes sceptically and proactively requested, 'Mum, please don't organise me! Can you please leave me to my own preparations?' I reluctantly agreed.

It was May and the mid-year exams were close. I had kept my promise not to interfere. Occasionally I asked Jett if he needed any help, and he assured me that everything was in order. When I checked in again – 'So, the exams must be getting close. How are you doing with your preparations?' – Jett reassured me that the timetable had been issued and he was working to his plan.

One Sunday evening, after a full weekend of rugby and basketball games and shopping for X-Box games, we were finishing dinner when my husband Ken enquired casually, 'Jett, your mother tells me your exams are close and you are all set for them. Is that right?'

Jett nodded. 'Yes, Dad.'

'When do they start, Jett?'

'Tomorrow, Dad.'

My husband looked in utter disbelief at his son, who gazed back at him calmly. Ken had spent his school career cramming at the eleventh hour, swotting through summary sheets and scrambling through reams of papers as a short cut because time was not on his side. It worked for him. He invariably ended up a little bit battered from the stress but with good results.

Unlike me. I was the anally retentive control freak who worked to a minute-by-minute study schedule. I was well prepared at least a week before exam week hit. I sat at the table glowing with pride as I looked at Jett, secretly thinking, 'Good on you, son. You must be just like me. Only better – because despite my preparation I was never as calm and relaxed as you are.'

My reverie was shattered with the next exchange.

'What have you been doing all weekend? Sports,

shopping, shooting aliens on X-Box . . . I have not seen you with any of your school books all weekend. Where are your books?' Ken ranted.

'At school, Dad,' Jett replied evenly.

'Where are your summary sheets?' Ken was getting more upset.

Jett remained calm. 'Didn't do them, Dad.'

Ken lost it. He started to lecture Jett about his disappointment, about not continuing to pay his private school fees and taking him out of school if his results were anything but A-grade. He threw his arms up and walked out.

As Jett and I cleared away the dishes, I asked him what he had been doing. 'I trusted you to study on your own without my organising you. Your dad is upset that you abused our trust,' I said.

'I have studied,' Jett said, 'just not in the way Dad expected me to. I worked out a schedule with my teacher and I understand my work. We have been going through sample test papers and I feel ready. My teacher told me to relax before the exam and so I did this weekend.'

A few weeks later, Jett returned with results that were impressive to say the least.

The moral of the story: Jett taught us a third way of exam prep – how to remain relaxed before exams and still get awesome results.

Parenting is leadership

Leadership is not easy. It takes practice. It takes time and effort to develop. Hence it is important to consider this: why do you want to lead?

For me, the answer to that question is the learning partnership – the number one leadership lesson from the home. Learning partnerships develop leadership self-awareness, adaptability and delegation. Here's an example that shows exactly what I mean.

Xian displayed assertive skills at three years of age that I would die to have at forty-five. She is so congruent with what she believes that she is willing to be punished to stay on her chosen path. By contrast, I had difficulty expressing how I felt when I was in my teens and it has taken many personal development programs to help me express myself. Xian, on the other hand, had no problem with that and by the time she was nine not only knew what she wanted, but she put a complicated plan into place to make sure she got it.

She had started ballet lessons six years earlier and was doing extremely well. One day, she sat me down and told me that she needed a break from ballet because she was exhausted from her many extracurricular activities and it was impacting on her focus at school. When did this young lady get so articulate? I asked whether she could eliminate other activities from her schedule – such as violin, piano, singing, gymnastics, choir, ensemble? Yes, she had already decided to stop choir in the new term.

She enjoyed gym and argued that this would help her remain flexible, strong and creative even without ballet. When I said I would talk to the ballet school principal, Xian assured me that she had done so already and everything was in order for her to stop next term – pending my confirming it with the principal. Can you beat that for assertiveness? Guess what? When I spoke to the principal, I found she was right behind Xian taking a break for a couple of years and returning again when she was ready.

Have you ever noticed that what we repress as parents is more than likely expressed in one of our children? My mother has often told me that I will be visited by what I most need to learn from my kids. How right she is! I could take a few tips from Xian in negotiating and getting exactly what she wanted.

Of course the greatest motivator for leadership in a family is the need to ensure the best for your tribe. Hence, the need to lead them down the 'right' path. You want the best for your lot, don't you?

What if I asked you to sum up, in two words or less, what you want most for your children? If you are like the hundreds of Australian parents Professor Martin Seligman has asked, you will respond with words like 'happiness', 'confidence', 'contentment', 'balance', 'good stuff', 'kindness', 'health', 'satisfaction' . . . and the like. In short, well-being.

And if I asked, 'What do schools teach?', if you are like other Australians you will give answers such as 'achievement', 'thinking skills', 'success', 'conformity', 'literacy', 'maths', 'discipline'. In short, accomplishment.

Notice that there is no overlap between the two lists.

Children's education is about accomplishment, which is the avenue into the world of adult work. Seligman said, 'I am all for accomplishment, success, literacy, and discipline, but imagine if schools could, without compromising either, teach both the skills of well-being and the skills of achievement. Imagine positive education.'

It is worth imagining. Australia, like every wealthy nation on the planet, is suffering an epidemic of depression. Depression is about ten times more common now than it was fifty years ago. It now ravages teenagers: five decades ago the average age of first onset was about thirty – but now it is below fifteen. Suicide, particularly among young men, is alarmingly common.

Prosperity is usually equated with wealth. The time has come for a new prosperity, a prosperity that combines well-being with wealth. Learning to value this new prosperity must start early – in the formative years of schooling – and it is this new prosperity, kindled by positive education, that you can choose for your children.

Leadership from the heart is essentially about leading towards this prosperity.

There is a word of caution about happiness at all costs. We don't want spoilt children. It takes all due diligence to keep expecting our children to take ownership and responsibility for their actions and their behaviour. But it is truly the only way they will learn. When, as parents, we intervene to justify and excuse them, they remain children. I remember a school principal telling me that a parent volunteered to take her child's detention because the child was unwell that day. We are our children's advocate but not their fall guy. They must be allowed to take full responsibility for their actions. To take it on the chin. To learn to be graceful when it is indeed unfair. We may need to be careful not to 'rescue' our children from life's lessons too quickly. Rescuing is less painful in the short term – but in the longer term, it may disempower them.

To be a great leader takes courage to sometimes stand back and watch those we love fail.

THREE

Leadership in Action

When my children entered the world with their respective destinies, my anxiety about being the 'perfect' parent was alleviated when I realised that I was less the sophisticated 'mother of superior knowledge' and more the awkward 'tour guide for Planet Earth'.

'Be the tour guide by all means' is the expectation. But it needs to be tempered with a good dose of reality. *Help us keep the schedule*, our children might say, *but don't take the surprise away by giving us all the answers ahead of time. Get us on the bus to continue the tour together, but feel free to humour us if we want to take an unscheduled stop to enjoy the sights. Remember to enjoy the tour with us. Don't stand by and let this be just a duty, nor let it be 'old hat'. Don't watch life go by. Live your life with us. Show us what you love so that we may*

learn about you and what you hold as true and good.
Leave a legacy of letting us live a life we love and hold
as true and good.

In other words, lead a great and authentic life yourself.
Let it be a grand experience for the whole tribe. Leave a
legacy for the tribe to do the same. And a word of caution: beware of trying to 'do it right'.

Doing it right

Think of all the times when we hold out the expectation
to 'do it right'. It can be about others doing it right. It
could be about yourself. If I were given a dollar for every
time a 'do it right' thought crosses my mind, I would
surely be a billionaire today.

In parenting, I was so fearful about not living up to
the standards my parents had set that it almost stopped
me from having any children.

The pattern is as old as time. As children, we are
expected to do the right thing by our families. To save
face. To honour the family name. Respect our elders.
In school, we are taught the right way to read, to form
our letters, to hold a pencil, to write. We are expected to
follow the right career, marry the right person, produce
two-point-three offspring, bring them up the right way,
be a credit to society.

In society, we are expected to do the right thing by the
norms dictated by our culture. To do the right thing is to

belong. To do otherwise is to be cast out.

But there is a caveat to that: if you are extraordinarily successful by breaking the rules, then you are unique and worshipped for your talent to break away from the crowd. Provided you are successful, then it is right.

And rules and values change depending where we are. Let's take the example of the value of 'respect'. All over the world that is seen as important. But it is earned in different ways in different societies. In the United States, respect of an individual means to support and challenge him or her to stand above the crowd: celebrating achievements of one over many. In Australia, respect means to give everybody a fair go: creating a level playing field so everybody can equally share in the spoils without any one tall poppy standing out over others. In Japan, respect is earned when one strives and is victorious while honouring tradition, way of life and the community one represents, be it family, country or corporate organisation; when the Japanese hero wins, everybody he or she represents wins.

Recently I received a phone call that changed my life – and that of my family. It began as a way of assisting a colleague place a suitable person from my network onto their team and turned into a 'call to adventure' for me, à la the 'monomyth' or 'hero's journey' described by the mythologist Joseph Campbell.

When the call happens, the initial reaction is to refuse. It takes effort to change the status quo. But in order to lead with intent to inspire, you have to make the difficult choices: 'I want to put a ding on the universe,' as Apple founder Steve Jobs said. People who want to do that have to think differently – and be prepared to be thought of as one of the 'crazy ones'.

In this case, I was being offered an assignment of a lifetime in the Middle East. It challenged a few beliefs: that it's too much to ask three others (my husband and two kids) to drastically reinvent their stable lives for me; that it's too difficult to relocate a whole (reluctant) household to a new country and culture; that surely it is the husband who takes the lead and the wife follows; that if it's not broke, don't change it; that the kids are in great schools and I cannot be sure the schools over there will be as good or even better; that my business is at its peak here in Australia so why risk it by taking off to foreign lands?

After six weeks of deliberation and conversations with my husband and children, and working with their current schools and a community of colleagues and friends whom I trust and respect, I decided to accept the call.

It is amazing what happens when you say 'yes'. There seems to be a 'flow' where things seem more effortless than before. The spirit lifts and tasks do not seem heavy. My husband was excited to creatively tweak his work situation to help make this happen. The children's schools went beyond expectations to assist us with school applications and became sources of information and advice. Clients and business partners were innovative in their support and assistance with transitioning my role here.

Family and friends counselled that the epistemological stretch would grow our children beyond any experience they could get in their current education and situation. And, despite long waiting lists, my children got accepted into the schools of our choice with relative ease.

This Middle Eastern odyssey is the beginning of a whole new journey. I am concerned with the inevitable 'supreme ordeal' Joseph Campbell describes, which is up ahead. Yet I trust that I will receive enough 'gifts' and meet enough 'guides' along the way for me to face and conquer what lies before me. I am looking forward to opening up my senses and welcoming the learnings from unexpected quarters. I believe this as yet unexplored adventure is a great example of 'breaking rules' and stretching my comfort zone while honouring the values of adventure and learning.

The seven Rs

For the last decade, I've had the pleasure of working with both families and organisations. As I continued this work, the similarities became astounding.

Families succeed when they are led by good parenting, plus the application of a set of principles. This mix works when applied with fairness, consistency and – here's the challenging couple – wisdom and humanity.

The more I've worked with leadership teams not only in Australia but across the Asia–Pacific region, the more the same principles – again applied with fairness, consistency, wisdom and humanity – work in organisations. Over the years I have honed that understanding into a structure I call the 'seven Rs of leadership' in business. My 'aha' moment came when I realised that they were also the 'seven Rs of parenting'.

PART TWO

The Seven Rs of Parenting

FOUR

Role-modelling

Role-modelling is at the heart of parenting: it is essentially about setting an *ideal*, an *example* or a *pattern* of behaviour that is worthy of following. It has been said that behaviour is the highest form of communication: actions speak louder than words. A leader is expected to walk the talk. This is the central core of authentic leadership – and of being a playpal (remember the acronym on page 3: *P*ractising *L*eader *A*vidly *Y*earning *P*artnerships *A*t *L*earning).

Most parents attempt to set a good *example* for their children, although they may end up setting a bad one. An example is a precedent for imitation, either good or bad. Most parents find it easier to provide their children with a *model*, a person or thing that is to be followed or imitated because of its excellence in conduct or character.

Not all children regard their parents as an *ideal* to which they aspire – 'ideal' suggests an imagined perfection or a standard based upon a set of desirable qualities. But young people's lives often end up following the *pattern* established by their parents, meaning that their lives follow the same basic configuration or design.

Role-modelling is how your children will learn from you most – consciously and, mostly, unconsciously. Sociologist Morris Massey described three major periods of child development that show how role-modelling can impact them.

1. *The imprint period.* Up to the age of seven, we are like sponges, absorbing everything around us and accepting much of it as true, especially when it comes from our parents. The confusion and blind belief of this period can lead to the early formation of trauma and other deep problems. The critical thing during this time is to learn a sense of right and wrong, good and bad. This is a human construction that we nevertheless often assume would exist even if we were not here (which is an indication of how deeply imprinted it has become).

2. *The modelling period.* Between the ages of eight and thirteen, we copy people – often our own parents but also other people. Rather than blind acceptance, we are trying on things like a suit of clothes, to see how they feel. We may be very

impressed by religion or our teachers. You may remember being particularly influenced by junior school teachers who seemed so knowledgeable, and maybe even more knowledgeable than your parents.

3. *The socialisation period.* Between thirteen and twenty-one, we are very largely influenced by our peers. As we develop as individuals and look for ways to escape our earlier programming, we naturally turn to people who seem more like us. Other influences at these ages include the media, especially those parts which seem to resonate with the values of our peer groups.

Working through Massey's observations, think how often you have found your children 'mimicking' the behaviour *imprinted* from absorbing you. For example, have you heard your tone of voice and exact words being used by an older child to a younger sibling? Role-modelling as a parent is important to help your children develop in the formative pre-teen years. This foundation, the result of the role-modelling, will support the latter years of peer influence.

In identifying who I am as a role model, one of the first things I did was to clarify what I want to be remembered for in living my life. I had to take stock of what is my purpose, what is my vision and what are the values I stand for.

Setting your purpose

My purpose: To leave people, places, things better than I found them. I don't want to wait until the end of my life to say I have reached my purpose. Instead, every day I look for the opportunity to leave things better. It could be simply tidying up my desk, upgrading my filing system, deepening friendly relationships with the neighbours, giving a dog from the RSPCA a new home, helping my children validate their magic brain with mathematical games or finding new words to add to their vocabularies. Bliss occurs in small but frequent moments every day when I connect with my purpose.

At the end of each day, I attempt to count at least one thing that I have done that satisfied this purpose. Ken, Jett and Xian support me to be on purpose. We usually start the morning with the question 'How was your day today?' as if it had already occurred – and we are celebrating (and, hence, mentally rehearsing) what we would like the day to be. This is just a way of consciously setting an intention daily, and focusing our attention on the energy that we would like to purposefully flow into particular areas.

If you haven't already, you might choose to reflect on 'What is *your* purpose in life?' If you have yet to identify what that is, it may be a good idea to put some thought into it, because knowing yourself is an important basis of role-modelling. Have you also recognised how and where your purpose differs from or is aligned to that of your family?

Setting your vision

My vision: Lead a great life to leave a legacy of loving life to my children. This consists of a series of shifting 'finish lines' for me – different milestones that I set regularly to keep my vision alive. Leading a great life does not mean making grandiose changes on a global scale. To me, it could be simply having clean water, eating healthy food daily, being inspired by nature as I take my daily walk. Or I can set longer time-frames with outcomes that stretch me to go beyond where I am comfortable. For example, it could be to learn a new language to the level of a native speaker in three years.

Let me share with you a process that helps me re-set these milestones regularly. Simple and fun.

1. *Count your blessings.* Be grateful for events, both positive and negative. Map out your relevant past or present situation (events that are positive as well as negative). For example, I may look at what I have achieved to date (say, I have birthed and nurtured two extraordinary offspring) and also what has eluded me (say, publishing my first book on parenting).

2. *Dream big.* Draft out an ideal 'desired state' (and perhaps give it a time-frame such as one month, one year, ten years – whatever you choose is okay). Be clear and specific about what you see, hear, feel, taste, smell when you are at this point. (I call

this the 'finish line' scene in your movie script.) Often we aren't clear – so that when we cross the finish line we don't even know we are there! For example, I see myself at my book launch, signing copies, hearing 'congratulations' from my friends and family, feeling very proud that there are many people buying the book even before it is reviewed.

3. *Make it meaningful.* Notice the reason you want this finish line to occur in your movie – that is, the meaning and purpose it gives you. The 'why?' is important because it serves as propulsion fuel for your motivation to get the 'desired state'. For me, when my message of joyful learning partnerships in parenting reaches one billion people easily and economically – that will make me totally satisfied.

4. *Reality check.* Reflect on what could be the blocks and stops. What is stopping you now from getting from your present situation to the finish line? Is it skill? Is it lack of experience? Is it will? (Then you need to check point 3 above – is the reason 'why' strong enough to drive you forward?) Do you need more resources, such as a mentor, books, courses, time, money, effort, support or help from others? For me, right now, it is about getting my book read – and I am exploring many avenues – beyond the traditional routes. My greatest block to producing the book was myself. I kept drafting and re-drafting the text until a colleague, friend and author, Jan Roberts

(in the 1980s she wrote the bestselling series of books, *Better Babies*, which has been reprinted by two publishers), took the manuscript off me and helped me get it to a variety of sources. And Rosina Mladenovic encouraging me to write a chapter in her book *Inspired Children* has pushed me to express myself further.

5. *Reorganise.* It's time to put a realistic action plan together. Brainstorm a list. Then prioritise from the *first step.* My first step was to get the draft out there.

6. *Celebrate.* When you have taken the first step . . . *celebrate.* Then prioritise your next two or three actions (the original action plan you drafted may need to be tweaked as you work through the steps).

7. *Pause.* And validate a win – no matter how small! Celebrate when you cross the finish line.

8. *Take stock with gratitude.* Count your blessings. Then create the next finish line . . . and so we go on.

All this may seem like common sense, and many of you naturally do this already. If so, keep on doing it. As you become clearer about your vision and the milestones to get there, what are you learning about the individual visions of each member of your family? How are you partnering to support each achieving his or her vision? If there is any conflict between visions, how are you adjusting things to make it win–win for all parties? Can everyone work together towards a compelling 'family vision'?

And please remember, it's great to schedule time just to indulge in *you* – it's simply good for the body, mind and soul. If you do not replenish your batteries, how will you have the energy to lead your tribe?

In setting personal visions for each member of your family, you combine your purpose with a mental rehearsal of where you would like to get to. In this way, you can be on purpose during the journey there. In recognising the personal visions of each member of your family, you can mentally rehearse where you would all like to get to. In this way, you can combine your purpose with those of the others.

Here are some personal visions for each of my family members centred on our chosen passions: Ken in surgery, flying and music; Jett in music, science, basketball and IT; Xian in creative writing, reading, arts and crafts and singing, and me in food, wine, movies and conversations.

Our 'family vision' is about respecting the unleashing of each individual's potential with a support system that encourages and challenges us all. We find time to use our complementary talents and diverse perspectives to help each of us change for the better. Interestingly, Ken and I usually play the complementary roles of nurturer and challenger in different contexts: Ken at the sidelines of basketball will be the one pushing hard to coax the winning streak out of Jett, and when Jett comes off beaten, I attempt the gentler 'So what did you learn from that?'

On the other hand, I will be the one to challenge Xian to take the bus to school on her own, whereas Ken usually relents and drives her there.

Some of you may already have a 'life vision' for yourself. If you have yet to define one, it could be useful to create a mind map, picture, prose or poetry that describes this vision using as many of the senses as possible. A visually compelling, rhythmically stimulating vision pitched at the appropriate emotional level can inspire you to mentally rehearse the taste and smell of your success.

Once you have a vision, the next step is to work out the milestones in getting there.

Working out your values

My values: These are the deep-seated emotional responses that drive me. They can be vastly different for everyone and can also alter from time to time. For example, when I was a single career woman, 'achievement', 'challenge', 'perfection' and 'freedom' were the most important values that drove me. After becoming a mother, my values shifted. Most important to me now are 'love', 'gratitude', 'connection', 'collaboration', 'learning', 'accomplishment', 'pleasure' and 'wisdom'.

The first step to being personally fulfilled is to understand the values that satisfy you, and how they may change from time to time. Have you contemplated the values of you and your family lately?

Eliciting values and understanding the differences for each of the family members are important. Satisfying your own values so that you contribute to how the family defines success – as a whole, as well as in parts – is key. For instance, Ken may value *achievement* strongly, while I consider *collaboration* important. So, when I support Ken to set 'stretch goals' and encourage him to achieve them, both our values are concurrently fulfilled.

I do not suggest for a moment that it is easy to align or satisfy everyone's values. But awareness is a great step to understanding and working together in your diversity.

If you are already aware of the values of all your family members, how similar and how different are they? How are each of you satisfying your own values and, at the same time, supporting one another in achieving theirs?

How does it work?

Let's explore some practical examples of what role-modelling on a daily basis could be like – and how my own values play out in this.

1. *Time for self.* I set aside ten minutes for yoga postures every morning, and ten to thirty minutes for a walk, bath or a read – and the children respect that to be my time, with no exceptions. This is when my values on gratitude and pleasure are satisfied.

2. *Balanced eating*. We eat healthy home-cooked meals most of the time – seated at the table together. We honour 'the team that plays together, stays together'. Here are my values about love and connection playing out. We permit fun foods too – after all, 'forbidden fruit' tastes sweetest. So we have a motto of eating everything we want in moderation. My belief: 'Whatever is repressed is expressed.' There really is no contraband and therefore any possible 'forbidden fruit' loses its fascination. We even have a set time every week when you can eat all the lollies you want in one sitting.

3. *Music appreciation*. From birth my children have listened to a spectrum of music, from Wolfgang Amadeus Mozart to George Michael. I wanted them to tune in to my world. In the last few years, Jett and Xian have introduced me to their musical world of Taylor Swift, Usher, Jay Sean, Jason Mraz and *High School Musical*. I believe that in keeping to the same wavelength range, we can continue to keep our channels of communications open. Can you see my values of collaboration, learning and connection coming through?

4. *Continuous learning*. My husband and I continue to attend courses regularly, both for professional and personal development. We also encourage our children to attend courses outside their usual school curriculum – for example, we took them out of school to attend the 14th International Conference

on Thinking in Kuala Lumpur with us and when they returned to school they presented what they learned to their teachers and peers. We signed them up for the Junior Leadership program when we both attended the Australian Annual Convention of the National Speakers Association. Ah, the joys of learning, accomplishment and wisdom.

In leading a great life as role models, we hope our family will do as we do rather than do as we say. Of course, their lives may be quite different from ours. However, our hope is that our legacy is one that encourages them to have lives of purpose, vision and values that are true to them.

Can you think of who was the first powerful influence in your life? I would not be surprised if it happens to be a parent or carer. Wouldn't you like to be the initial most impactful influence in your child's life?

As a leader and a learning partner, notice what other role models may have impacted you. My great-grandma, who I knew for less than a decade, taught me three things as a role model:

1. Strength to strive and thrive: 'When the going gets tough, the tough get going.'
2. Self-belief: 'Don't let being a girl get in the way of being the best I can be.'
3. Self-drive: 'If it's going to be, it's up to me.'

What have you learned from your role model(s) that has made you who you are?

The 'think–do–get' model

There are two models that may help you track and understand 'how you do you' as a role model, or when you are studying the role models you want to learn from.

The 'think–do–get' model is a structured way of looking at role-modelling. It starts with loosening and 'losing your minds' – those preconceived notions and judgements that lock you into robotic reactions – so that you become more mindful and aware (*think*) of self and others. Then it is about 'coming to your senses' so that you read the sensory data coming in – and therefore interpret it objectively in its right context so that you can frame or re-frame it for the outcomes you hope to achieve. Essentially, this is about being organised with a clear, inspiring vision/plan that needs to be communicated and implemented (*do*) in order to achieve the purpose, vision or results you set out to *get*.

THINK ⟹ DO ⟹ GET

If you expect your children to fulfil their dreams, live their passions and reach their highest potential – in other words, live a great life – then you need to role model this expectation.

Behaviour is the highest form of communication. If you do not live what you say, then don't say it. You cannot tell the next generation how to live their lives. You show them by example. For instance, many of you expect your kids to practise their piano concertos by Mozart and listen to their Suzuki violin pieces regularly so they can excel at making beautiful music. Yet some of you have never even attempted to play the recorder or sing a single Christmas carol or attend a classical music concert, let alone tune in to classical music on the radio or buy some music by one of the great composers. That is sending incongruent messages to your young ones.

In other words, as practising leaders, what do you do to show your family that you are on purpose and living your passions at the highest level? The clearer you are about your beliefs and values, and the more self-aware you are, the better you will be in communicating that to your tribe.

Being aware of your 'allowable' weaknesses is useful. You can help your tribe step up to significance by showing enough without becoming an episode from *Jerry Springer*. For example, I am not a morning person and my time management is harried at best. In order to get everybody out of the door in time for school, I have let my kids in on a secret: as much as we all like to think I am Supermum – well, I'm not. So we have a new time captain in Xian. She gives us a countdown two minutes before we have to be out of the house. It works pretty well for everyone. Xian feels significant, Mum feel authentic, there is less need for Dad to play *24*'s Jack Bauer shouting

'Go! Go! Go!', Jett feels relaxed and everybody gets to school or work on time.

And to be a great role model, you need to fulfil yourself: to 'do' in order to 'get'. I was feeling guilty about going back to work after three years of my 'opt-out-of-career' sabbatical. My family side was fulfilled, but I was not satisfied on the professional front. 'If I expect my children to unleash their highest potential,' I thought, 'what am I doing to realise my own?' So I went back to work – not as a dentist, but through forging a new path in leadership facilitation. It was not an easy road. Yet I was inspired – by my children – to do what I love, to follow my passion, to persist in learning a new craft. It is about practising my (self-)leadership.

Think of what you are role-modelling: do you feel you have lived up to your expectations of yourself? If so, how? If not, how will you choose to do so differently?

The Matrix and role-modelling

Perhaps there are those of you who are fascinated – like I am – by how we are 'doing' or 'being' ourselves. In navigating the role-modelling aspect of knowing myself, I became fascinated by a movie.

Most of us have watched *The Matrix*. Recently, I revisited the movie and remembered how, in my parenthood role, my current coaching and facilitation work and previously as a dental professional, I have been fascinated by the amazing matrices I have navigated with my family, clients and patients.

In *The Matrix* is a 'world that's been pulled down over our eyes to hide us from the truth . . . It is a prison of our mind . . . a neural-interactive simulation, a dream world that we live in, the inside of the map, not the territory.' The main character, Neo, is invited by Morpheus to take a red pill to learn the truth about reality or to take a blue pill and live in blissful ignorance.

So, what would you say if I propose that every one of us lives in a unique matrix that identifies the individual as a multi-dimensional system of dynamic self-organising neuro-interactive frames – and that is how we create our sense of reality? Seems like science fiction or Alice-in-Wonderland stuff? If you wish to pursue this further and 'follow the White Rabbit', take the red pill and read on. If not, then take the blue pill and stop right here.

The Matrix as a model

When you develop models, you do so in order that they help you navigate your various experiences. No model is real or absolute. No model is 'the truth'. Models are just maps that you can use to go exploring. So is the matrix model.

Dr L. Michael Hall developed his 'neuro-semantic matrix' model to provide a way to map human meaning-making and experiencing so that you can more easily find the critical frame for change and transformation. It provides a way to profile experiences; model best practices and expertise; suggest steps to replicate excellence; refine and reframe meanings, and design new frames for higher quality living, loving and contributing. As a model, the matrix allows you to enter into your own or another's matrix to learn and recognise the frames in action. This is useful in tracking the role-modelling process in more detail.

What relevance has this for your home tribe? Parents set up the best environment for family members to facilitate their physical, emotional and spiritual development and to create the most resourceful lifestyle habits (such as diet, hygiene, exercise, stress management, routines, manners, traditions and beliefs).

Imagine how useful it is to be able to enter each individual's matrix so that you may understand your children or co-parent better, and also help them to transform their health, well-being and self-esteem easily and elegantly.

You can navigate the matrices of any tribal member in order to understand your learning partners better. And imagine what it would be like to be able to discover more about yourself by journeying through your own matrix to understand what makes you brilliant and where you could be even better?

The human matrix

According to Dr Hall, we are all born into a matrix of frames of reference for thinking and feeling. These frames are incorporated into the language we learn, the family into which we are born, the culture that we assimilate, and the education that guides what and how we learn. These social realities serve as the cultural matrix, or womb, into which we are born. Inside all the cultural frames of beliefs, values and expectations, our mind and emotions are 'cultures' and 'cultivated' so that we are fitted for life in a given social reality. For example, some of us may have entered the professions of law, finance or healthcare because the culture into which we were born nurtured individuals to learn a profession at a university in order to have a secure financial future.

In addition, each of us invents and creates a matrix of frames that governs our sense of reality. We build these frames from the experiences we have, and we continue to construct frames as we seek to understand and experience new things. Some people in management may have constructed beliefs about sales teams generally being motivated by financial rewards, and therefore think there is no point in engaging them in any other kind of way. Or you may identify yourself as the 'expert' – and so you end up micromanaging every tribal member up, down and around you. What power or resources do you, as parents, perceive as having (or not) in order to be able to change your teenager's moody behaviour?

The human matrix is 'the reality' that you live in. It is the reality that results from all your models and maps, memories and imaginings, fears and hopes, that give structure and form to your life. It emerges from the social frames you inherited and from the ones you invented. All these frames of reference and frames of meaning make up the matrix you live in, and from which you engage the world of people and things. This is the world as you know it from the inside.

So what is your world constructed of? Is your identity in your professional or business life different or exactly the same as the one your family, golfing buddies, wealth creation network, health club and spiritual community would recognise? Step back, reflect and notice these nuances in your world.

Breaking down the matrix

Hall designed the matrix model as a 'womb' of meaning frames and definitions. In other words, the matrix is comprised of submatrices. All these frames, embedded within frames, make up the essence of your personality, your attitudes and your perceptions. They govern who you are and what you are about. They are built around your mind–body–emotion states, and they come from developmental psychology, particularly from Erick Erickson's work about the psychosocial stages of human development.

Your *state* is hence the foundational matrix that grounds all your frames, and with *meaning/value* and *intention/purpose* make up the three *process matrices*. There are also five *content matrices*: *self*, *power* (or *resourcefulness*), *time*, *others* (or *relationship*) and *world*.

From the meanings, intentions and states that you create and experience, you construct meanings about specific subjects. The particular content about some things are so critical that they determine the very feel and fabric of reality for you.

For instance, parents who are highly apprehensive about the safety of their family have constructed a reality around the *meaning* of the world being hostile, and their *intention* is to avoid any contact with strangers or to ensure that their children are always in familiar and secure surroundings, and they get into a *state* of high anxiety every time they even think about the prospect of their children venturing into a different community or becoming involved in new activities.

The *self* they identify as a parent is one of protector of their helpless children; their *power* in that situation is the familiar and therefore they perceive new people and untried circumstances as events in which they have a total lack of control or resources; they feel unable to speed up the *time* when the children will be grown-up and independent; they perceive non-family members as the *others* who are dangerous and punishing rather than partners in a social partnership; and the *world* of parenting to them is frightening and one in which they are inexperienced and unskilled.

It would be interesting to explore the individual matrices of such parents to help them deal with new experiences for themselves and their families more resourcefully.

Consider your work tribe. First, look at the process matrices: middle managers' *meaning* of work is about results, their *intention* is to look at the bottom line, profit, productivity and efficiency, and they are in a *state* of high anxiety every quarter reviewing key performance indicators in their line of business. Then consider their content matrices: their identity of *self* is one of a 'meat in the sandwich' caught in between frontline and senior leadership; their *power* in that situation is that of 'being torn' both ways; they feel utterly *time* poor; they perceive senior leadership and their direct reports as the *others*, who are pulling them in all directions and it's difficult to please both; and they see the *world* of business as a battlefield of daily fighting, crises, limited resources and troops to manage.

It would be useful to navigate the matrix of such managers to help them deal with their challenges of execution more effectively.

On a more positive note: what if you, as parent, had the *meaning* of learning partnerships in your families, the *intention* of looking for opportunities to learn from your co-parent and your children, and you are in a *state* of curiosity and wonderment? With the identity of *self* as one of an authentic leader, your *power* is that of 'being myself with more skill' who can understand and meet the needs of your tribe; you feel *time* is now and being present in the moment; you perceive all the tribal members (immediate and extended) as *others* who are excited partners acting with significance and community towards a common vision; and the *world* of diverse personalities in the tribe, when understood, have purpose, values and vision aligned. What would that be like?

The matrix and you

To begin navigating your own matrix, step back and reflect:

State
- What are you thinking and feeling right now?
- How intense is this state of mind, emotion or body for you?
- Do you have a name for this particular state?
- How do you get yourself into this state?

Meaning/value
- What does this situation, event or the person/people in it mean to you?
- What and how much significance do you give this?
- What is the quality of this meaning?

Intention
- What is important to you? Why?
- What do you really, really want?
- When you get this, what does it do for you or what do you get from it?
- For what purpose do you want this?

Self
- What are you like? How do you define yourself?
- How valuable do you think you are as a person?
- Do you set conditions on your self-value?
- Does this self-value support and enhance your life?

Power

- What natural talents do you have?
- What mental, emotional and behavioural skills are you confident about?
- What skills do you need to further develop and refine?
- Do you have the ability to produce a desired or intended result?

Time

- Is time your friend or enemy?
- What time zone do you normally live in: the past, present or future?
- Do you have the ability to manage time effectively?
- Are you able to step out of time and enjoy the eternal moment when you so choose?

Others

- What audience do you carry in your mind and play your life to (for example, your parents, friends or some group you aspire to belong to)?
- Do you regard your audience as open, friendly and rewarding, or are they fearful, dangerous and punishing?
- Do you easily enter a trusting relationship or hold back?
- How much of a team player are you?
- What are your best social and interpersonal skills and states?

World
- What do you think about life and the human adventure?
- Is the universe friendly or frightening?
- What specific worlds (for example, arts, friendship, learning, finance, sports, computers, business, leadership, parenting, religion, parapsychology) captivate your interest and fascination?
- What worlds do you never explore?

Although the matrix model seems to be all around you, it is actually a world of your own making and construction. In fact, you invent as you go. Every day you add belief frames, value frames, understanding frames, decision frames, intention frames.

So what would your matrix be like if you were a playpal?

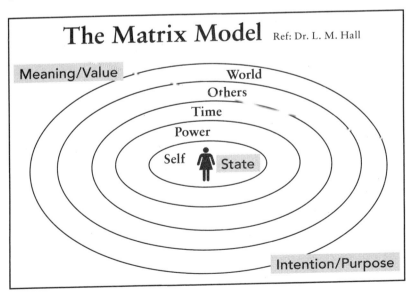

The Matrix Model Ref: Dr. L. M. Hall

Meaning/Value

World
Others
Time
Power
Self State

Intention/Purpose

Entering the matrix

When you meet someone, their matrix is invisible. When you say 'hello' and the other person returns the greeting, the matrix is activated. The response you get tells you the first little bit about the frames and the matrix of frames in which the other person lives and operates from. Matrices are invisible until they are activated. Navigating each other's matrices becomes important for playpals as you co-create learning partnerships that are useful and constructive.

The further you go into the matrix (whether your own or that of another) and the more information you receive, the more of the matrix of frames you activate. This allows you to see the world inside another person and the universe of meaning that creates emotional life.

You enter another's matrix by matching and mirroring what you receive from that person, validating their reality so that he or she feels heard, understood and safe. It is the sense of safety and not being attacked or judged that allows you to enter another's matrix. If you offer anything that sounds remotely like attack, judgement, criticism or rejection, then the matrix will close to you.

With your own matrix, you enter through acceptance and even appreciation as you respectfully acknowledge your frames and seek first to understand. This means seeing and hearing that reality for whatever it is.

Seek to enter the matrix – whether your own or that of another – rather than fight it. How? By respecting it and honouring the person rather than judging or feeling contempt for her or him. Fighting the matrix means that you don't understand – that you are blocking yourself off from the other person (or from your own self) – and that elicits defensiveness so the matrix will not show itself. Then you become self-blind and unable to be aware of or understand another person.

Through recognising and respecting you understand that everybody's matrix is unique. No two matrices are alike.

Paradoxically, it is through welcoming and embracing the mystery of your matrix that you are able to transform it. How can you tell when you are in the presence of a very different matrix? Listen for the language of uniqueness:

'I just can't get inside his head.'

'I don't know where she's coming from.'

'I wish I knew what makes him tick. It's a mystery to me.'

'I can't relate to her. Was she born on a different planet?'

Making the matrix work for you

How do you use the matrix?

Essentially, for the self, it is a useful exploratory tool of self-awareness, discovery, acceptance and appreciation. As Socrates said, 'Know yourself for the truth will set you free.'

The matrix model is also a very useful tool to explore

the achievements of extraordinary performers in any context, industry or profession – be it sports, business, wealth creation, research, coaching, medicine, dentistry, child prodigies or other parents – in an effort to replicate their stellar experiences and achievements in your own lives. Imagine what it would be like to track and unpack the matrices of successful entrepreneurs such as Richard Branson, Anita Roddick or Oprah Winfrey or brilliant minds like Stephen Hawking or Albert Einstein or the artistic genius of Margot Fonteyn, Fred Astaire, Ginger Rogers, Charlie Chaplin, or the extraordinary leadership of Mahatma Gandhi, Nelson Mandela, Aung San Suu Kyi or Margaret Thatcher? Is there someone you can model as an exemplary playpal?

Consider what you can do to enter and appreciate the matrix of each of your tribe's members (whether in the family, business or community context), respecting their values, beliefs and identities so that you can instigate longer lasting changes in their lives through authentic role-modelling and learning partnerships.

Entering the matrix is essentially about tolerance, acceptance and appreciation. It is about making your world one of more choices through awareness and respect of one another's matrices. It is about celebrating what is great and unique about each one of you and deciding to transform that which you prefer not to be, do or have.

What have you done to continuously improve your self-awareness and to incorporate that into your daily life? Go on. Follow the White Rabbit further and see what you find in your matrix.

Live your voice: Walk your talk.
Live your vision: Be your word.
Live your values: To thine self be true.

The three Rs of partnering skills

The ultimate aim is not for you, as parents, to have a tribe consisting of mini-versions of yourselves running around. And I am not suggesting that the kids will pick up exactly what you consider to be important. Think about it: how many of your parents' behavioural traits have you consciously rebelled against? Probably the exact ones they wished you to emulate. That's life.

What I am suggesting is this: as a role model, live the best life according to you – not the life you think you *should* live. Love life. Lead a great life. Leave a legacy so that your children will too: in their own way. Role-model your passion. Isn't that what passion spells: 'pass-I-on'?

When you are a consistent and authentic open 'book' as a role model, how much easier and clearer is it for your children to:

1. *Read* you: to look, listen and learn what you value, what you love, what is meaningful to you.

2. *Right* it: adjust it for their context in order to benefit them in *their* lives.
3. *Re-write* it: to make it authentic and purposeful for themselves – to love and live a great life – according to *them*.

How are you being your own best playpal role model for your tribe? What are you doing every day to lead a great life as a role model? How will this give your family a legacy that may in turn help them to love and live a life true to them?

Dos & don'ts

Do look at what your identity is as a parent

What is your identity? I-have-all-the-answers, student of life, rescuer, giver, control freak, doormat, dictator, conspirator, co-navigator, captain, coach, teacher, motivator, fairy, wizard, collaborator, CEO, researcher, homo sapien, caretaker, tour guide, bus driver? The role you unconsciously fall into sets up the mindset by which the family is run. The beliefs or values congruent to this identity surface, resulting in corresponding behaviours. For example, a rescuer 'mollycoddles' and does everything for the children so that independence and other tough lessons of life may be delayed in them – when the rescuer can no longer protect the kids, imagine the consequences of them trying to deal with the harsh realities of life.

Do be yourself – more – with skill

What energises you to be engaged with your leader? You trust them to be themselves, and yet be able to adapt skilfully to changing environments. Simply like an authentic chameleon. Effective leaders are credible and accomplished in your eyes, and somehow they make you feel significant enough too. That's what parents as leaders are. Proponents of tough love. Ruthlessly compassionate. Vulnerable and comfortable with your origins.

What does it take to be an effective leader? As the leadership experts Rob Goffee and Gareth Jones conclude: 'Be yourself – more – with skill.' Go figure, parents.

Do lead a great life

Do that for yourself – and you are encouraging your children to be the best they can be. It all starts with you. A lot of parents intuitively 'sacrifice' themselves so that their children can have it better. Let's go counterintuitive. Imagine if you, as a parent, aspire to, and fulfil, your highest potential. What message are you sending to your kids? Behaviour, after all, is the highest form of communication. What better way is there to encourage your children towards their highest potential than through this role-modelling?

How do you transform tomorrow's leaders today? You start with yourself. Excite your own self to exceptional performance, and your children too will be themselves – more – with skill.

Don't be hard on yourself

Lessons are learned when you admit that there is no failure – only feedback. Try it a different way. Small tweaks can make huge differences. If Wile E. Coyote would just revisit *one* of his ingenious ways to catch the Road Runner . . .

Personal learning journal

What have you done to continuously improve your self-awareness and to share that improvement with those you love every day of your life? List at least two examples.

1.

2.

Think of your own role model: do you feel you have lived up to your expectation of yourself? If so, how? If not, how will you choose to do so?

Do you feel you are a good role model for your children? If yes, then why?

1.

2.

3.

4.

If no, then why not?

1.

2.

3.

4.

List at least one thing you have learned about yourself from this lesson?

1.

Write down at least one action you will implement immediately.

1.

FIVE

Respect

You select role models, consciously or not, because you respect these people enough to want to emulate some of their qualities. Successful role models leave such a legacy by example, so it must be that they respect themselves as well as others. Let's examine what respect means.

Respect is to regard someone or something with admiration, esteem and reverence. It can be accorded anyone because of their abilities, qualities and/or achievements – not necessarily just because of their title, position or chronological age. You 'love' to hold in high esteem a particular person who arouses and draws forth the best in you and in others. Your respect for that person invites inspiration.

A child affording respect to the parent seems obvious.

Should the parent respect the child? Absolutely. Children may be younger, have gained fewer accolades and seem less experienced in their worldliness from sheer lack of years on the planet. However, they certainly earn my respect for their untarnished ability to navigate with complete curiosity and wide-eyed wonderment in infinite contexts, and they possess an extraordinary ability to maintain a high-performing learning state with a total can-do, never-say-die attitude (a case in point: all babies fall down umpteen times and never give up learning to walk).

Let's explore two ways where you can show respect:

1. Keeping your word.
2. Exploring the perspective of others.

Keeping your word

Respect in its daily manifestations is as simple as keeping your part of the bargain. I believe it is important to 'be my word' to everyone – regardless of age or social status. I take care not to renege on promises. How often have you promised your children a play in the park and then it gets too dark or cold to go out and you change your mind? Surely that is a sensible decision – and plans can be adapted. But it is how you explain this decision to your children that demonstrates respect, or not. Respect means to re-negotiate what you do together – and not to cancel the play altogether 'because I said so'. That is more like bullying, which I am sure you would rather not role-model to your children. Offer an alternative instead – perhaps a conversation by the fireplace about a book you are reading together, or playing billiards or table tennis indoors.

Exploring their perspective

Children naturally yearn to learn from grown-ups – after all, adults were in the playground first! It is much more counterintuitive to learn from your kids.

Children are not apprenticed to *become* human beings. I believe them to be quite complete entities, and they are probably closer to the source of spirituality and purity than any grown-ups can attest. As an adult, you increasingly argue for your limitations, and you seek to validate these as you move on in the world over the years. You continue to burden the children with more and more constraining beliefs in the name of protecting them: it starts with the word 'no!' when they begin to expand their experiences beyond what you term 'safe'. How often have you lost the opportunity to partner with them, to learn from and negotiate their perspective – and together reason out if it is indeed an issue about safety? Are you teaching them fear instead? Would it not be more respectful to explore their genius (or possibly demonstrate their folly) early through discussion first?

Think of someone you admired and respected when you were a wee child, one of your early positive role models perhaps. I remember a neighbour from when I was hardly five years old. She was a young architect and loved drawing pictures for my sisters and me. They were usually fashion-type sketches of beautiful women wearing fantastic outfits. What amazed me was how she encouraged *us* to draw. She made us feel as if we were the greatest artists! I learned to draw a lot of figures – and constructed my first 'paper dolls' – through her inspiration. Because of her respect for our creativity, we produced a profusion of 'fashion' drawings that we sent to relatives around the world with pride. The mutual respect for one another was evident. I believe this nurtured a learning partnership between the architect and the young artists in us. She taught us how to draw and she sparked our interest in art. In turn, we showed her novel ways to depict figures and fashion!

My children revel in the messages from *The Little Prince* by Antoine de Saint-Exupery and Richard Bach's *Jonathan Livingstone Seagull*, both of which applaud the expansive viewpoint of the young, and emphasise the self-inflicted limitations of grown-ups. In defending these adult limitations, you impose your thinking on your young rather than stand back with respect and non-judgement to listen to their refreshing perspective. In sharing these stories, you ponder the possibilities of a wonderful world where grown-ups consistently respect and hold the young in high regard.

How does it work?

What are some everyday instances of respect in families? This is a sample of how our family has attempted to exemplify respect.

1. *Pause before we say 'no!'* When I cannot understand why my children are making a choice to do something I disapprove of, I have found it useful to pause and reflect on whether it is possible to see it from their viewpoint. Then, when I can still see no good reason for their choice, I ask them why they want to do it. Believe it or not, I have never failed to learn something. I never let the opportunity slip without sharing my non-judgemental perspective, and show respect enough to check if they would like to hear what I have been thinking. As we all know, kids are consistently curious. So they will usually ask me to share. Bless their souls! My hope and belief is that our children will usually learn something from us at that point. It may be stored for future reference – and may well be their version of 'what not to do' – but still it is a learning point. This is what learning partnerships are all about. I believe we explore more possibilities together this way – so that we can work out a solution that is far better than just pushing a singular agenda.

2. *Exercise our understanding, not our position.*

Beware of using the demotivational phrase 'because I said so' from your parental position. An authentic leader does not sway from his or her intent. At the same time, a leader without followers is no leader. How do you excite your followers to exceptional behaviours so they are burning with exhilaration to realise your intent? The key is: respect your followers by knowing what motivates them, and thus meet their needs while achieving your intent. How? Once again, it is about coming in early as a learning partner – not late as a judge. Like any typical mother, I dreamed of Xian learning ballet, but she had other ideas. When she quit ballet after enjoying it for six years – and doing very well at it – my instinct was to activate the 'because I said so' option, but I stopped myself in time to learn the reason for her decision. I had to step back and reflect on why I wanted her to continue with ballet. For me, it was the artistic and fitness factors, and my joy at watching her dance. But she satisfied two out of three of my criteria – by continuing with gymnastics and music – and I enjoyed watching her doing her gym routines anyway. Once again, this typifies a win–win, mutually respectful learning partnership. In exercising my understanding rather than my position, we were both happy with what ensued.

3. *Code of behaviour*. The foundation of respect is a clear charter or code of agreed behaviours that

parents can communicate to younger children. With older children, it is good to re-negotiate any behaviours that may no longer apply – or which may have been unforeseen. For example, behaviours involving potty training will no longer be applicable for a teenager, but boundaries around, say, driving and staying out late with friends may need to be set.

4. *Keeping your word.* When a promise has been made – such as going to a certain movie together, baking, reading – it is honoured. If it has to be postponed or changed, it is re-negotiated. I don't know about you, but there are busy days when I simply haven't the energy (or the inspiration) to tell Xian a story at bedtime, so I cuddle up with her and have a long conversation instead. It serves as a variation on story-telling, because, in reality, it is exchanging each other's stories. We also enjoy exploring a story we've read together: what the characters are like, how they behave and what the philosophy of the story is.

5. *Respecting choices.* I have a coaching client who respects her daughter's choice of clothes, and so avoids any battle about what her daughter wears daily. The caveat they have agreed is that my client gets to pick clothes for special family occasions, such as weddings, funerals, birthdays and Christmas. Seems fair, don't you think?

I wonder if you too can recount how you inspire respect from your children, and how you have shown them respect.

Respect is not automatic. It is earned. In order for your tribe to respect you, you have to show them respect. So what can you *be* to inspire their respect?

How often have you promised your children a compelling reward and then reneged on it, at your convenience. For example, I have heard of carers telling children, 'When you have packed up your toys, we will go for a walk.' So the kids get organised, and then are told, 'It's got too dark now. Maybe another day.' Without even an acknowledgement of how well they have fulfilled their part of the bargain. It is not fair!

Is it any wonder that communications start to deteriorate as the years roll by because grown-ups do not show the basic respect of simply just keeping their word.

One of the things I am really aware of is what I promise my children. On most days, after homework is completed, we will go for a walk with our dog Mitch – go out in nature, pick flowers, rollerblade or casterboard – so they always look forward to that. But what if it rains, or I get caught up in a conversation on the telephone and it gets dark? Do I say to Jett and Xian, 'Too bad, it's dark, it's cold, it's raining – we won't go for a walk right now.' Or do I take them out in the rain and let them catch a cold? What do I do?

Out of respect, as I would with any of my adult friends or family, I'd say, 'I'm sorry I got caught up in that phone call. I can't help that it's raining, but can I suggest that rather than going out in the rain and getting colds, we do it tomorrow for twice as long? And I'll make sure that I won't take any phone calls then. Right now, how about we sit and play Monopoly together?' My children usually start with disappointed looks, but quickly brighten up when a favourite board game is mentioned – we may play Uno or Snakes and Ladders or work on a puzzle. So I have changed the game from walking to something else. Yet the value of spending time together is uncompromised. I have negotiated a respectful relationship.

'Being' (or keeping) our word is a simple way of showing respect. Sure, there are times when plans need to be changed because of altered circumstances. Again, the children at least deserve an explanation of how and why things have changed – and plans have had to be postponed – and perhaps you can get their input about when, what or how they would like it made up. For example, in the situation described above, when it is getting too dark to go for a promised walk, you could show your appreciation of their efforts in keeping up their part of the deal, and then ask, 'It is getting too dark to go out so what else can we do instead of the walk? Shall we postpone it to first thing tomorrow? Or would you prefer to do something indoors together now – say, like telling stories by the fire?'

In business life, such negotiations may not be as obvious as that. However, you often have to shelve projects, cut resources or pull rewards or incentives following instructions from higher levels. In those situations, how have you shown appreciation or validation of where your team has got to before the changes came into play? Have you taken the time to celebrate wins (no matter how small) up to that point? How have you elicited ideas from the team to deal with the changes to show that you respect their points of view? And how does that parallel what happens in the family when the world around you turns topsy-turvy unexpectedly?

Self-respect

Then there is the self-respect of standing up for what you believe in and its importance if you are a role model. For example, you may tell your children that you hold honesty as a high value, but then when you get pulled up by the traffic police for speeding, you tell a fib about how fast you were going – in full earshot of your little ones.

When I was deciding to hang up my dental drill, I wanted to respect my father, who had sponsored my university education while I was studying for my dental degree. My father reminded me what he told me when I was seventeen and undecided about which tertiary course to enrol in – 'If you love what you do, everything else follows: happiness, money, status' – and, he said, it still applied to my decision to move to leadership facilitation and coaching. Ultimately, it was my father validating my self-respect by realising that there was a vocation I was more passionate about, and so I needed no permission from him to pursue it. That's a great learning partnership.

When the oxygen mask falls from overhead in an aviation emergency, you put the mask over your head first before attending to others. You need to look after yourself first before you can look after others. Likewise, self-respect needs to be role-modelled. The children see me take time out every morning for yoga, for a walk or for a coffee with my girlfriends – we need to set time for the self to rejuvenate and recharge. The children are given 'golden time' to do as they please daily, once homework, chores and music practice are complete. They can play Nintendo, watch television, read, Skype their friends and cousins or skate in the park.

So how honest are you with your family? Are you living your values, and walking your talk? Do you have enough self-respect to be a role model for your tribe? Do you give your family the opportunity to show respect to you?

Respect through rapport

In parenting, rapport is really important to build trust and respect. A leader without rapport is like a sailing boat without wind: you may have the vessel, but it is unlikely to get where you are planning to go.

Rapport – being in harmony – occurs through

building similarities at the *unconscious* level. I wonder if you can remember a time when you tried so hard to be in rapport with your children that you agreed with them so overtly that they became suspicious and irritated because it seemed as if you were mimicking or being condescending. A big part of what business professionals do is build relationships with their customers. No matter how superior the product or technical expertise is, ultimately you are people dealing with other people. Unless you are in rapport with your customers, they are unlikely to take your advice. After all, most of us don't like taking guidance unless it is from a friend, a trusted colleague or a professional we respect and like.

Building rapport between people in any relationship can be defined as trust, being on the same wavelength or showing mutual respect. If it is not happening 'naturally' then it may be necessary to construct it systematically.

Rapport occurs without conscious attention between good friends, close allies and comfortable acquaintances. When all is well you do not need rapport-building skills. Learning these skills becomes necessary when a relationship is not going well, when you have disagreements with friends or colleagues, when people are different to you, when you appear to have nothing in common. Rapport-building skills are a must when you don't 'like' a person – have you ever had customers, colleagues or team members that fit this bill?

People who are like each other usually like each other.

People who don't like each other have their attention drawn to the differences between them.

The process of rapport building involves *pacing* and *leading*.

Pacing means to connect and create trust by building similarities in order to establish a 'bridge' of commonality between two or more people, without the other person being consciously aware of what you are doing. Matching or mirroring the rhythm and pitch of the conversation, the common ground of ideas and perspectives or the posture and energy of the other person are examples of pacing. Pacing with the intention of respect and honouring the other person creates rapport. They will feel understood.

To develop or take the relationship in a particular direction, leading needs to occur. The test of rapport is when the other person follows your lead. Leading is changing your behaviour so the other person follows. Rapport needs to be established before leading will be effective. You cannot lead someone over a bridge before first building it.

If the other person does not follow your lead, it is an indication of insufficient pacing. Any resistance is a sign of insufficient rapport – for example, your child raising objections to your proposal of how to complete a school project.

The more you apply some of these seemingly simple ideas day to day, the more quickly you will notice the transformation in your leadership skills and in your tribe of influence. Pacing and leading are respectful ways to motivate your kids, help relate better to your significant other, and persuade and influence all those meaningful people in your personal and professional lives. They are essential tools in winning any argument and still being liked. They allow you to negotiate any deal, get what you want and still have a good relationship with the other party. Persuade and influence with integrity. Communicate with ease, eloquence and elegance.

Respect through suggestion over direction

Have you ever told your child of the best career option for him or her to pursue? After all, 'Mother/Father knows best, right?' Wrong. If your child has definite ideas to the contrary, it is likely to be an uphill effort on your part to convince otherwise. More often than not, your child ends up vehemently opposing the recommended option. However, if the suggestion seemed to develop from the child's own thinking during discussion, then your idea tends to be easily and unanimously agreed upon. Seems obvious, does it not?

Being openly bossy all the time can be disrespectful. So how important is it to mind your language as parents or leaders?

It is all about being suggestive. The key to success begins with building and maintaining rapport. It is imperative to remember to pace the world model of the person you are communicating with. Speak their language. View things from their perspective. Step into their shoes. Be empathetic.

Once you are in rapport, you can more easily lead them with your suggestions.

The idea is not to impose your suggestions. Allow them to make meaning for themselves. Personalise and engage the person with artfully vague language as you seamlessly weave your suggestions in.

What is meant by being *artfully vague*?

Try this exercise. Think of a happy occasion in your life. It may be something that happened as recently as yesterday, last week or maybe last year. Or it could be an event when you were a child, like a birthday party or some other celebration. A milestone in your life. Notice what you are seeing, the sensations you are feeling and the sounds that are all around. Perhaps there may be some memorable smells. Or indelible tastes. Relive this happy event and, as you do, notice how uplifting it makes you feel right now.

What happened for you?

I am quite certain that the happy occasion I referred to is vague enough so that every one of you who took part in this exercise would have experienced or remembered a very different event that is unique and personal. Yet it seemed like I was describing a happy occasion specific for each person. That is being artfully vague.

Even the suggestion to 'notice how uplifting it makes you feel right now' remains artfully vague enough to be special for each person. Recognise that it is not about forcing or telling someone what to do. Rather, suggestive language is much more invitational. Otherwise, there could be a tendency for the listener to reject your suggestions.

This is exceptional rapport building because the speaker and the listener are both seemingly on the same journey, expressed through artfully vague suggestive language.

Here are several more examples.

- Dealing with a young nail-biter who is approaching her seventh birthday: 'I know your father and mother have been asking you, Sally, to quit biting your nails. They don't seem to know that you will naturally quit biting your nails just before you're seven years old. They really don't know that! So when they tell you to stop biting your nails, just ignore them!' The more Sally enjoys biting her nails to irritate her parents, the more she reinforces the suggestion that she will give up nail-biting. In this double-bind, the rational mind has no way out: *You're damned if you do, and you're damned if you don't.*
- We are all familiar with this typical technique for closing a sale: '*Would that be by credit card or cash?*' The question presupposes that the customer is settling the account regardless – hence the sale is virtually done and it's just a matter of the method of payment.

- How about the manager who suggests, *'Would you like to take your overtime on this project or on the next?'* When the employee picks either, he or she is committed to doing overtime on at least one project.

As you are probably realising, these language patterns are nothing unusual. You are already using suggestive language in your day-to-day living. You just didn't know it up until now. Being aware of this allows you to use it proactively, in quite a conversational manner, to get the results you intend. You may even attempt something a trifle more complex.

- Let's say you have a teenager who finds it difficult remembering instructions. How about saying: *'Try very hard not to remember what I'm about to say to you.'* This statement contains an *embedded command* – a sophisticated technique to demonstrate *everyday hypnosis*. While the conscious mind is trying to cope with what it hears as a command – to forget what it has not yet heard – the unconscious not only hears the suggestion of failure in the word 'try' but may also hear the command: *'Remember what I am about to say to you.'* For this command to register, the speaker must *mark* this phrase by speaking these words with an unexpected inflection, by pausing before them, or by associating them with a gesture.

- *Negative commands:* How often have you heard parents shouting out the order: 'Don't touch that!' And what does the young one do? Invariably, she or he touches the forbidden item. Why does the child disobey the command? The reason simply is that the brain cannot 'not do'. The spurious negative in the phrase does not get computed. For instance, if you are told, *'Do not think of a pink elephant!'* what do you do? You immediately form a visual representation of a pink elephant in your mind. Similarly, in the child's mind, the idea of 'Touch that!' has formed and is followed through as if that were the supposed command – much to the dismay of the parents. So when you next attempt to remove a plaster from a child's healing scab, do avoid the usual 'This will not hurt' routine. You are creating a representation in the child's neurology of what it is like to hurt. Instead, you could say something like, 'Let's see how little you feel this.' The next time a member of your team is attempting to learn a new skill, I wonder what it would be like to say, *'Don't do it right, just give it your best shot'*?
- We can respectfully ask quality questions with more precision to clarify and to show genuine interest. Generative questions (questions that generate solutions or options) can be used in problem-solving situations to pop the listener's thinking to a whole new level of processing to acquire new perspectives.

- *Reframing* is an elegant way of assisting a person to make new meaning in circumstances they are currently perceiving as negative or not serving them.

Being conscious of your language patterns day to day is a respectful way of communicating.

Applying the three Rs of partnering skills

In order for both learning partners – parent and child – to understand and respect one another, and therefore be able to relate easily, consider using these skills:

1. *Reading*: open up your sensory channels to observe what is the 'world' according to the other – see, hear, feel, smell and taste it as if you were them.
2. *Righting*: if unclear, get it 'right' by clarifying through questions, then, when there is trust and rapport between you, offer insights to them about how it is in your 'world'.
3. *Re-write: help one another reframe any difficult situation* by suggesting a new way of experiencing it or possibly a new way of thinking about it.

How are you being respectful to yourself and your tribe with ease, eloquence and elegance?

Dos and don'ts

Do engage in richer relationships with your child(ren) at all ages

Expect nothing but to *be present* with them. By doing so, you learn from them as much as they learn from you. Have you noticed how present children are?

Do lead and learn from your children

When you are effective leaders as parents, you make your children better leaders. After all, children learn best by role-modelling behaviours. Besides, leadership is not hierarchical. If your children can excite you as parents to exceptional performances, that makes them the leaders. Babies learn to lead you to get *whatever* they want from the time of birth, right? Playpals come in all shapes and sizes.

Don't be set in your own ways

Being interested in what your children think or how they do something opens up new possibilities of you learning new and possibly better approaches to any situation Curiosity breeds innovation.

Personal learning journal

Write down how you respect your children/tribe.

1.

2.

3.

4.

Write down thoughts and feelings you had from this lesson.

1.

2.

3.

4.

Write down at least one thing you will implement immediately.

1.

SIX

Rules

R espbecting self and others is crucial. Respect needs to arise from understanding rather than fear. Mutual respect can come from observing rules.

How can you respect rules?

Why have rules?

Let's look at sporting rules. They provide structure and directions for the game. The players understand the rules, know the purpose of the game, how to compete safely and that there are consequences if the rules are broken. There are different rules for different roles in the game: the goalkeeper, the quarterback (gridiron) and centre-forward (netball) all play to different rules – and at different places such as a soccer pitch, a football field or a netball court.

The purpose of rules in the family is similar to the

above. The rules set boundaries and a structure by which every family member agrees to behave in different contexts. There are safety rules, such as young children holding hands when crossing the road, driving rules and safe sex rules for young adults. In some families, there are specific rules for each gender, or according to order of birth (this is quite common in some cultures). Rules may vary depending on different family locations, occasions or contexts – for example, some families have strict attire to wear for Sunday church service, weddings or funerals.

Relevance

A rule needs to be relevant: there should be a reason why it is important. For example, why road rules? It could be about safety. Why bedtime rules? It could entail getting into a healthy routine.

Some rules come from traditions handed down over generations. Others have been created by the individual family. This is when the partnering of parents and children becomes important. To work properly, all rules, whether handed down or newly created, need to be agreed to by family members.

Sometimes it is necessary to do some revision. One Gen Y child challenged an old family tradition and was promptly told, 'We've always done it this way.' Not to be put off, our young investigator found out that great-great-great-great-great-great-grandma had a very small oven – which was why all the limbs of a turkey had to be removed so it could fit into the oven. The following Thanksgiving, the turkey graced the table with all its limbs intact.

Moral of the story: rules that are no longer relevant or useful need to be reworked, revamped or refined.

How does it work?

Some examples of rules that have served our family well include:

1. *Food*. There are 'everyday' foods and 'sometimes' foods. Healthy eating is encouraged with 'everyday' vegetables, fruits, nuts, water and fresh fish or meat any day. But there are 'treats' such as lollies, chocolates, cream cakes, soft drinks (and wine for adults) that we have 'sometimes' on special occasions, according to the family charter. For example, we have 'lollie happy hour' on Fridays from 3 to 4pm and soft drinks on Saturdays, 'school holiday treats' such as cream cakes and ice slushies, and Christmas pudding.
2. *Sleep times*. Bedtimes on weekends and holidays are more relaxed than on schooldays, when a curfew takes effect after a specified time.
3. *Exceptions*. What if a birthday falls on a Thursday? Does that mean no lollies (it's not Friday

'happy hour') or Sprite (it's not Saturday) or choc-olate mudcake (it's not the school holidays)? Well, this would be a festival special – like Christmas, Thanksgiving, weddings, graduation – where excep-tions are acceptable.

4. *Changing rules.* We rewrite some rules so that they are current and fit us better. For example, our safety rule of 'hold hands when crossing the road' became obsolete for Jett and Xian once they had reached a certain age, and it has been replaced by 'stay alert when crossing roads'.

5. *Charter of agreement.* Our family has a 'civil code' in which we agree that there is to be no physical violence (such as hitting, throwing things at others, and so on) or verbal abuse (screaming expletives, calling names, etc). The consequences for breaking the code are time out for the number of minutes that match the offender's age (for example, a three-year-old would get a three-minute time out; a sixty-year-old grandma would get sixty min-utes – and, believe me, this happened once in our household when a child gave Grandma a time out for screaming!).

6. *Frequent good behaviour points.* FGBP – better known in our family as the GBF (Good Behaviour Fairy) – is a system of collected points awarded to one another by members of the family, which is claimable for a product or service (a 'goal' set ahead of time, such as a Nintendo game worth

seventy dollars, could mean working up thirty-five points to get it). It works like this: taking the initiative (say, offering help to a sibling so the latter awards the points) is worth two points; but if they had to be reminded to do something (say, I had to remind them to brush teeth before bedtime) they would only earn one point. Conversely, if a behaviour is deemed undesirable (for example, a child leaves toys in the living area when the agreement is to respect common areas), then he or she may lose two points. Why the GBF? Well, all good fairies (like Santa's elves) know when you are pouting, sleeping, naughty or nice – so, inevitably, a special bonus gift can miraculously appear under the pillow from the Good Behaviour Fairy when the points keep growing. Since it is the fairy's gift, the big thrill is that there is no need to redeem any points in this instance. The system is also inflation-proof and GFC-protected.

What rules have you agreed to with your family? What current rules are no longer useful and what new rules have you consciously chosen to replace these with? How have you partnered with your children to co-create and agree to these rules?

We have looked at rules which you are conscious of. Could there be any rules you are unaware of that may be driving your behaviours?

Unconscious rules

Rules can also be beliefs that drive you unconsciously. When brought to conscious awareness, they become useful tools to create the future you want.

What is known about beliefs and how they work comes from the great wellspring of knowledge that is thousands of years old, spanning Chinese, Greek and Roman philosophies, and brought up to date with a particular synthesis of that material into cognitive behavioural therapy by Albert Ellis, in the mid 1950s. More recent additions to belief theory and belief change work include the books of Robert Dilts, published over nearly two decades. However, we owe perhaps more to the writings of Epictetus (55–135CE) and the modern decoding of still older wisdom about personality by the Native American Thunder Strikes working with Jan Orsi in the book *The Song of the Deer*, published in 1999.

These unconscious rules are ingrained beliefs that may have been useful and served us in the past. They make up the mindset we default to under crisis. Ken remembers that when he came home with a school report one time, the first thing his parents focused on was not the As he received, or the 98 per cent in maths. Instead the question was, 'What happened to the 2 per cent you got wrong in maths?' No doubt it helped him get better by looking at what he got wrong and correcting it. However, over time, the rule became less useful because Ken started downgrading his amazing achievements by focusing on the near misses. That can be demoralising.

Since this is the mindset we default to under crisis, as parents this was one rule we decided to re-engineer. When Jett brought back a maths quiz with a score of 96 per cent, Ken made a conscious effort not to look for 'What did you not get right?' – which puts the focus on the 4 per cent that were answered incorrectly. Instead, what positive reinforcement it was for Jett when his father encouraged him by zooming in and asking, 'How did you get those 96 per cent right?' We noticed his excited sparkly eyes as he told us how he could improve on that and conquer the missing 4 per cent next time around! We were all energised by his response and engagement. In fact, I believe I learned a new way of looking at things.

Some unconscious rules that our family has found useful to adopt:

1. *Energy flows where your attention goes.* Encouraging our children to focus on what works and what they are good at means they count and do more of that. This creates a successful upward spiral (rather than a vicious downward one) and results in more counting and less discounting. It is important to celebrate even small tweaks, small successes, and to not dwell too long on lessons learned before moving on.
2. *There is no failure, only feedback.* Let us accept that not everything works to plan. It is a learning

experience to tweak and do things differently next time – so experiment, encourage and expect improvements (no matter how slight or gradual). Keep moving forward – for example, when Jett or Xian solves seven mathematics problems out of ten, we ask them to look at what they did to get the seven right. We then ask whether they could look at the three that did not hit the mark and see if what worked with the seven could have been applied to those three. Time and again, they then work out how to solve those – and so improve their score the next time. Mostly it is carelessness rather than lack of understanding. So we can acknowledge that and the learning to focus better next time.

What rules do you currently live by that are no longer useful, and which may actually be limiting you? What new rules have you consciously chosen to replace these in order to be more empowering?

Rules can empower

When I was a child there were a lot of school rules. I used to think 'Rules are terrible – when I am a mother there will be no rules!' Big mistake. No rules means the children don't know the boundaries. Every time they do something they need to ask me. How tiresome!

So we sat down to work out some rules together. Here's how negotiations happened when my kids were five and seven years of age.

Mummy's rules

Rule 1: Homework first before play. 'It's very important to Mummy that you finish your homework first because I care that you don't get into trouble with your teacher, and I care that you learn so that you may teach me some things too.'

Rule 2: The common area in the house is to be kept tidy. 'We are sharing the living space, parents are not perennial hired help in the service of the god of childhood and I want to spend time with you playing rather than cleaning the house.'

Kids' rules

Rule 1: Activities with Mum after homework – for example, go for a walk or play games.

Rule 2: A story at bedtime.

Xian at five years old was the one who told her older brother Jett to put things away. Perhaps she was learning delegation as a leader. Now Jett is the one who is the more tidy of the two. Friends come over and wonder how I manage a tidy household. It's nice to be able to say that I have two little helpers.

If the children know the rules it is much easier to keep the boundaries. Boundaries are important to everyone. When these are clearly defined, it allows for independence. When you have rules, you have freedom. Funny that.

Freedom and self-discipline are two sides of the same coin. You need to have both happening at the same time to achieve independence and fulfilment. How? If given a few simple rules to follow, then you know the limits within that context so you can act independently within those confines, knowing that you do not have to keep checking with the person in charge, whether it is a parent, a nanny/caregiver or teacher.

If there are no rules, you are caught in the prison of uncertainty. Nobody likes that. Besides, I don't want to be the nagging mother pointing my finger all the time. That would make me always the bad guy. With rules, you lead your children to freedom. That's love, isn't it?

I remember 'observing' at my children's pre-school and kindergarten. It is the Montessori School philosophy to encourage parents/carers to come and 'observe' prior to entry and during the duration of the children's enrolment in the school. As I sat down, I was given a one-page guide on how to conduct myself during the thirty minutes I had been allocated. I welcomed this succinct little document as I was able to be like the metaphorical 'fly on the wall' as the children went about their work undisturbed.

Knowing the rules meant I did not intrude on the children's work space in the very limited time I was there.

For example, I was not to speak to any of the children unless they came up to me and initiated the conversation. (I discovered later that the culture in the classroom is not to seek to ask an adult questions – especially a visitor – and to attempt to do things on their own first. 'Help me help myself' is a great motto in the school.)

Keeping to the guidelines, I was able to efficiently and effectively observe the many goings-on in this class of two dozen or so three- to six-year-olds, which gave me a good snapshot of the philosophy of the school. There was amazing industry, quiet focus, a respect for each other's work and the mentoring of the younger ones by the older children. The director (not 'teacher') floated among them doing her presentations (not 'lessons').

Some of these simple rules included: let each person focus on his or her own work without being disturbed; join in only if invited; all unfinished work to be labelled with names so the person can return to it the following day; when work is completed, all implements must be put back exactly where they were found to respect the next person using them.

Agreeing on a code of behaviour allows for independence. Children know there are consistent consequences as a result of not honouring the agreement, and because they understand the expectations clearly they are empowered to act without constantly having to check for permission.

Our family's civil code, which covers the principles of behaviour we expect, is written on a poster board and covers both rewards for good behaviour (tracked via our

GBF point system) and the consequences of misdemeanours (such as the length of time out and the systematic deduction of 'good behaviour' points). It is important to reinforce desirable behaviour through validation, celebration (no matter how small a win) and counting (versus discounting) any small tweaks of continuous improvement. There is also a section on safety rules describing how to act in 'emergency' situations such as in case of fire (what to do, who to call and where to congregate).

What do you do with your family to co-create rules that are clear enough so you do not have to micromanage? What rules do you observe with your family? Are the rules written down? Do they include any exceptions? What other rules would you like to add?

Making meaning is making rules

Making meaning – thinking rationally – is the ability human beings have been endowed with over the rest of the animal kingdom. An event can occur in your life and, depending on what meaning (another unconscious rule) you make of it, could create emotional havoc, elation or you could feel nothing at all.

When I was at my first job straight out of dental school, I was so grateful to be employed, I fell in love with every aspect of life at work – everything was viewed through rose-tinted glasses. So what if the practice manager yelled at me for spending too long with each patient?

I reckoned she was only trying to keep the next patient from waiting, and to give me feedback about speeding things up. So what if I only had patients scheduled from 8 to 9.30am, and then from 3.30 until 6.30pm? These were the busiest times after all and I was there to support the overflow.

When one is in love, life is beautiful. I focused on all the positive things in the job and chose to ignore whatever was not.

Things remained the same in the practice for another six months. Sure, I started to get more patients and more hours scheduled – from 8 until 10am and another half hour in the afternoon. My skills had accelerated along with the pace – and I religiously kept appointment schedules on time even though I still made a point of getting to know every patient. Despite my most conscientious efforts, the practice manager continued to behave like a sergeant-major, barking constantly, 'This is not a social club . . . we have work to do here.'

And then, something inside me just clicked. I began to give new meaning to these events. I wanted to be busier and to be treated with more respect. When I realised these little aspirations were not being fulfilled, my initial thoughts slowly grew into a sense of resentment towards the workplace itself. Before long, any chance I could, I left the office for an extended lunch between 11am and 2.30pm. I started to nit-pick about all the things that were not working. I had fallen out of love. Within three months of that revelation, I resigned. Meaning: I was looking at everything to justify why I could not or should not stay. So I didn't.

Change the meaning, change the rule

Six-year-old Jett was looking forward to his first day in Year 1. Most other kids had started in the kindergarten at the school. Jett was the new boy. I can imagine his excitement: new uniform, new school facilities and, of course, new friends. He was up early that morning, dressed himself, packed his lunch into his new schoolbag and was too excited to eat breakfast. Boy, was he pumped!

It was a different Jett I picked up from the school later that day. 'So how was it?' I asked the boy, who had lost all traces of that glowing exuberance. Jett said, with tears brimming, 'It was such a long day, Mummy. I cried today because I missed you.' It broke my heart. Then I thought about it: he was the only new boy in the class and was in an unfamiliar environment with a system of doing things that was totally different from the one in his kindergarten. He knew no one in the class. It dawned on me that the same things that had stirred such excited anticipation in this child were now causing him anxiety. The event of going to a new school remained the same. However, the meaning had changed.

The next morning he woke up early because he was too anxious to sleep. He still could not eat breakfast as he was anxious about missing me that day. I needed to help him create a more resourceful and tangible meaning to get him through the day at school.

I asked if there was any way that he could still miss me and feel good. Jett told me that he missed me because he cares about me. Caring about me felt good but it made him feel sad because I was not there physically. I suggested that when he thought of me and started to care and hence miss me, it actually made me feel sad to know that he was feeling sad. So it would help me feel better if he looked for something to do that would make him feel good in order to overcome the sadness. Jett said that a few of the children and the teachers always came up when he cried. So instead of crying, he would tell one of them that he was missing me and needed help to play, do something or just talk about it. Together we had co-created a new meaning with which he now could deal with this issue.

Obvious efforts can be made to change your own meaning, or unconscious rule, about seemingly difficult situations you face in life, as Jett has demonstrated by recognising the problem and overcoming it.

Jett settled into school. He still missed me but his teachers told me that the tearful episodes were shorter and practically nonexistent. He began to focus more on his work and was more inclined to communicate his feelings.

A few weeks later, he wrote a short note that summarised the change in his attitude towards the new environment: 'Mummy and Daddy, thank you for letting me come to this great school.'

Change the meaning, change the rule: Jett appreciated this change.

The meaning of change

What is change, really? It is not something empirical – you cannot see, taste, smell, hear or feel change. Change is really a process that alters, modifies or transforms a thing – and essentially describes the difference between a beginning state and an end state.

You hear of people being excited about change – say, about moving into a new home, getting a promotion or experiencing a new culture. Then there are moments when you fear change – new responsibilities on the job, learning to cope in a new environment. Once again, the events could well be similar – and your emotional responses to them could be so different.

Messages in the media and the prevalent cultures seem to suggest that today's generation encourage and welcome changes rather than not. Today, it seems that if you stay in a job for more than three years, you are a 'stick in the mud' – and run the risk of being unflatteringly labelled as an 'under-achiever', 'insecure' or a 'loser'. The message is loud and clear: if you feel that you are undervalued, paid less than you think you deserve, not advancing at the pace you desire – you develop yourself by moving on. Change is good.

Such notions are in stark contrast with the work ethic

that was held in high regard fifty years ago. Back then, happiness was a job at a very big company: the organisation man left home, spiritually as well as physically, to take the vows of the company. The man (and it was almost always a man – few women had careers) had to pretty much marry the company, usually right out of university, and after a brief interview had settled their careers for life. This was the golden age of job stability, or the grim slog of stultifying conformity. Again, depending on what meaning you make of it, tradition reigned supreme. Change was bad.

Is change good or bad? I truly believe it is neither – it just *is*. Change happens. You put your meaning to it – and respond accordingly.

So is it possible to consciously change the rules, or beliefs, that drive your behaviours? Let's explore the possibility through a few processes.

Changing rules

As was illustrated above, unspoken rules may be limiting beliefs that are no longer useful in your lives. Becoming aware of these rules of your subconscious – and changing or rewriting them to become more empowering – is an exercise that you can do with your family or your team.

Some rules are so ingrained that they dwell in your subconscious and drive your behaviours, programming you into a patterned response. These rules are your beliefs. It could be that little voice in your head that tells you such things as 'I must not test fate,' 'I am from a poor family so I will always be poor,' 'I was never clever at school so I will never be successful,' 'My boss is always right, I can't question him,' 'Don't stand out like a tall poppy,' and 'Stay with the crowd or you'll be cut down.'

Some of these rules may certainly have served you well. But what if they are no longer useful? How can you change the rules? Here are a few processes:

1. Changing rules through the ARC process.
2. Changing rules through re-patterning.
3. Changing rules from mandatory to choice.
4. Changing rules through minding your language.

Changing rules through the ARC model

Let us explore a model called the ARC process.

Adversity – Identify adverse situation in life

Rules – What (old) rule(s) caused this pain?

Example 1

Adversity: I was not allowed to do that although my older brother was given permission.

Possible rules: I am not good enough. I am too young. I am just a girl.

Consequences: I can't do that so why bother trying to ask my parents for anything? I'll rebel and go covert.

Example 2

Adversity: My child's level of reading is below the average in his class.

Possible rules: My child is not good at reading.

Consequences: I tell him to focus on something else he is good at. His reading does not improve.

It is illogical to keep doing the same thing and expect a different result. What do you need to do to change the results in your life? Change the rules. How can you do this?

Let's take the examples earlier and apply this change:

Apply – Alter (old) rule in similar adversity

Rules – What (new) rules to adopt?

Change Life – How will life be now?

Example 1

Adversity: I was not allowed to do that although my older brother was given permission.

New rules: I can show my parents that I am worthy of trust despite my age/gender.

Possible change: I build my case and then ask my parents for permission.

Example 2

Adversity: My child's level of reading is below the average in his class.

New rules: Every child can read – each takes a different time-frame to get there.

Possible change: I encourage my child by noticing what kind of story he likes and get more books like that. I focus on strengths, and ask directed questions to meet his needs. My child loves reading.

The ARC process helps you change your thinking to change what you 'do' in order to 'get' a different result.

THINK ⟹ DO ⟹ GET
MUSCLE MEMORY

So how can you use ARC yourself and with your teams?

Example 3

Adversity: I have not sought further promotion in the company because I am uncomfortable with leading people, especially my peers.

Old rule: I am too old to learn new skills such as people management and leadership.

Consequences: I stay in a position that has hardly changed. I am bored. I gripe a lot.

New rule: I have enough experience with working on projects at church all my life, and bringing up four great kids – so how hard can leading a team of old friends be?

Possible change: I make time with HR to discuss how I can take the next step up.

Changing rules through re-patterning

In one research project three groups of college basketball players of similar skill were studied over a given period. One group practised shooting hoops every afternoon. The second group was asked to imagine shooting hoops without attending the courts. The control group played cards. The results? The skills of the control group had actually worsened. The first group improved a little. But there was a phenomenal change in the second group. Not only had they improved their rate of shooting hoops over the other two groups, but as they sat there imagining shooting hoops, the muscles they would use to shoot hoops were firing as if they were physically doing so.

The explanation? It's about mindset and muscle memory.

The first group were shooting hoops and there were times they missed. But the second group had a 100 per cent success rate because in their imagination they were successful every time. And as they imagined the ball going in, their muscles were firing. Their mindset ('think') creates a muscle memory ('do') which, when repeated, creates an anchor for a successful result ('get'). With enough frequency, intensity and duration, a new rule is patterned.

In order to change a rule, you can create a reproducible gesture or a muscular movement with conviction – but you need to do it at least five times. Why five times? The linguist Noam Chomsky postulated that when we learn a language, we default to speaking with associated muscular movements, which in turn create certain neurological ruts. These neurological ruts, because they are the shortcut that your brain remembers, fire each time they encounter similar situations (for example, adversity in the ARC process), and activate the 'rule' that drives similar responses. You don't have to think about it – it's neurological. It's not logical. It just happens automatically.

In order to create a new pattern or re-pattern so you can change the consequences of the rules that drive you, you need to create a new neurological rut for yourself: whether it be learning a new language, shooting hoops or being an intellectual genius. Try it on.

The first time it happens in the brain, it is a happenstance.
The next time it happens, it is a coincidence.
The third time, it is a pattern.
The fourth time, it is inevitable.
The fifth time, it is a new rule – neurologically.

In sales training, the preference is to repeat something over seven times. That has to create a neurological rut – that is re-patterning.

The Suzuki method of learning music utilises the neurological rut process. Before the student plays the piece on an instrument, she or he listens to a recording of the piece being played perfectly over and over. Listening is part of the practice.

Don't take my word for it. Give it a go. Notice what new rules you can create through muscle memory re-patterning.

Changing rules from mandatory to choice

I was watching my children say goodbye to my husband one morning. It was my turn to take the kids to school as Ken had an early appointment.

Jett, who was five, remarked, 'Dad, do you have to go to work?'

'Yes, Jett,' Ken said. 'I have to go to work.'

Xian piped up. 'Why don't you want to stay and play with us, Daddy?'

Ken thought about it and then replied, 'You know what? Those are such great questions you have asked. Let me say it this way. Jett, it's not about "having to go to work". I choose to go to work now because I promised someone that I'll meet and work with her. I would also love to be with both of you, and so I promise to come home tonight at six o'clock to play then. Life is about making choices and the time to do them in, so we can do all that we love, with whomever we want to and when-ever we wish.'

Ken's reply worked like a charm. 'See you at six o'clock, Daddy!' the children chorused as they energetically waved their father off to his car. No tears and whining. Simply because they know their daddy always keeps his word. As for Ken, he had not a tinge of guilt for leaving his kids that morning. And why should he have? If anything, there should only be pride in keeping one's promise. To live as our word. The children are obviously proud of their daddy. And I am so proud of all of them.

That little morning scene often replays in my mind when I feel like I 'have to do' something, 'must be' somewhere, 'should be like' someone. It seems to me that we have been 'should-ing' ourselves into less than compromising situations, by being overly passive about making decisions. How did that happen? When did we start short-changing ourselves in the process of making choices?

So if you have been 'should-ing' yourself to do things, imposing a 'these are the ways we have to do things' mentality on yourself and laying the blame on external forces that 'make' you conform, then you are not being accountable and responsible for your own decisions and, by extension, for yourself. Things simply happen to you. You are just a victim. You are never the cause.

Conversely, you can choose to live by a different maxim: 'Life is about making choices and the time to do them in, so we can do all that we love, with whomever we want to, and whenever we wish.'

Changing rules through minding your language

Mind your language. We have often heard that saying. Why is that? Language is the map of your experience, which you represent or record in your minds. Can it be possible that if you change your language, you can change your mind – and in turn change your experiences? In other words, does your body respond to what you have in your mind?

Our bodies are listening

Let me propose that we are 'at cause' all the time. Let us also assume that the universe will conspire to achieve that which we can manifest.

I am therefore curious to know why we would manifest disease in ourselves. Ever wondered about that?

In the health arena, there are increasing statistics that show that autoimmune diseases (such as lupus and allergies) make up for more than 60 per cent of complaints in the community. Together with cancer, they make up the majority of diseases that we battle against.

Both cancer and autoimmune diseases have one thing in common: it seems the body is not fighting an external enemy (such as viruses, bacteria, fungi). The body is 'eating itself up' (in the case of lupus) or growing out of control (with cancer) – and, hence, seemingly attacking itself. Why is the body doing that?

Dare I conjecture that the body is fulfilling our

wishes? Let me propose that it is our thoughts and what we have in our minds that have brought forth that which has come about in our body. Here she goes now: talking about the mind–body thing, you say. I guess I am. And not least because mind–body medicine is fast becoming mainstream and gaining widespread acceptance.

Let me cite an example of children suffering from migraine headaches who have learned self-regulating strategies to deal with their chronic pain. Dr Karen Olness, professor of pediatrics at Case Western Reserve University in Cleveland, Ohio, has stated that 'although we don't know the specific cause of migraine, we do know from controlled studies that regularly practising a relaxation imagery exercise results in far fewer migraines than taking conventional medicine for the same purpose. Children trained in self-regulatory techniques did far better than the children with the medication, and certainly better than the children who were placebo, and received no treatment at all.'

In the case of Marette, who suffered from lupus and was being treated by a very toxic drug, Dr Olness used a 'cyberphysiology training strategy' as a means of controlling some aspect of her physiology or body processes. In order to reduce the drug dosage Marette that would require, Dr Olness created a 'conditioned response'. This means that when Marette was given the intravenous injection of the drug, she was simultaneously given cod liver oil and a sniff of a pungent rose perfume. Taste and smell have been shown in research to be the most easily conditioned senses – and so both were used to double the chances of success. After three pairings of the drug and the stimuli, Marette was given only the scent and cod liver oil. Because of the conditioning, her body reacted as if she were receiving the drug. The stimuli had elicited the correct physiological response so her body could fight the lupus but without the side effects of the drug.

Using self-hypnosis, biofeedback, meditation and relaxation imagery, Dr Herbert Benson, professor of medicine at Harvard University, has found, by measuring physiological responses such as temperature, heart rate, pulse or brain wave patterns, that the body has the ability to respond to the mind communicating with it.

Evidence-based 'mind over matter'? That's what it seems like.

The next time your mind thinks the following thoughts, beware what it is communicating to the body:

'Work is stressing me out.'
'This is eating me up.'
'She makes my blood boil.'
'I am under so much pressure.'
'I must do this even if it kills me.'
'This is a pain in the ass.'
'My life is out of control.'
'I wish there was some way I could slow down.'

So is it surprising that your body might respond with ulcers, elevated blood pressure, cancer, lupus, heart attack, piles or constipation? After all, you are giving your body a host of cyberphysiology training strategies to act upon.

In short, be careful what you ask for: your body is likely to deliver. Imagine if your body responds to your mind telling it to slow down. What is the best way to make that happen? Well, it seems you will not rest voluntarily, so let's create a way. Perhaps your body creates an opportunity for you to fall over and break a limb – that will surely slow you down! How about growing a malignant cancer – now you really must assess and prioritise what it is you truly want to do in the limited time you have.

Painful yet rewarding lesson

Several years ago, my colleague Bill was complaining of being very busy and, supposedly, it was beyond his control. He was doing so much: running two practices, volunteering in dental professional organisations at both state and federal level, and lecturing at the university and on the continuing education circuit. Something had to give. Guess what? His body decided to respond with Hodgkin's disease.

Although he has recovered well, the treatment he had to undergo prevented him from remaining a clinician. Bill had excellent income and disability insurance cover and he sold his two practices for what he considered to be a good price. He admitted that the cancer treatments –

radio- and chemotherapy – battered his body quite a bit and he certainly did not enjoy them. However, he loved being able to slow down and speak to the other patients when he was undergoing treatment. Perhaps that allowed him to reflect on what he enjoys doing the most.

His role in dentistry has changed: now it involves more corporate consultancy and continuing his service to the professional organisation. Yet some things remain the same. Bill is still busy – and loving it. I can't help but notice the changes in him: he has a more relaxed countenance and state of mind, which is pretty much the opposite of his previous self. He admits as much – for example, he finds himself living for the present, unlike before he became ill. Another one of life's little ironies, wouldn't you say?

It does appear as if circumstances have forced Bill to become a happier man. And the lesson? We need a congruent and clear action plan between our mind and body. I like to think of it as dancing to the same beat and rhythm.

If it is true that we can manifest our wishes, why not start with things we are passionate about and love to do? Let us be inspired with thoughts that will awaken all parts of the universe to conspire to create what we aspire to!

So, go ahead: Change those rules that no longer serve you.

The life-changing experience

Let me share with you some of my personal experience in this area.

When I was at the pinnacle of my dental career in private enterprise, I remember harbouring a secret desire to experience life-changing events in my pursuit of my 'true purpose'. All I knew was that my goals must have nothing to do with dentistry. Incidentally, that is exactly the kind of vague goal-setting problems that I warn people about these days.

During that time, I had become pregnant. My doctor congratulated me on the positive pregnancy test – Ken and I had been married for seven years and she knew we were hoping for such an outcome. But I was devastated. I burst into tears, sobbing, 'My life will never ever be the same again. How can I bring up another human being when I don't even know my own purpose in life?' First case of antenatal depression?

Pregnancy is definitely a life-changing event, although not exactly what I had in mind. Okay, I guess I should have been more specific in stating my secret wish. As it turned out, my body took me literally and decided that my secret wish – so secret I didn't even know it myself – was to become a mother. That's the power of the unconscious mind.

Two weeks later, I began to wonder whether, if I was fulfilling my 'life-changing experience' wish, it was also putting me on the path towards my true purpose. Such an idea certainly made me feel better. I decided to surrender myself to the hands of fate – come what may.

'Just hold the space'

Women speak of wellings of unconditional love during childbirth, as the baby pushes into the world – and I used to think that was Mother Nature's way of justifying the labour pains.

The delivery experience was slightly different in my case. Believe it or not, I experienced an urging from my unborn son even as he struggled to make his way into our world. 'Mum, don't stress yourself out about parenting me the right way. Don't worry. I have my own destiny – and nothing you do will change that. Just hold the space for me and I will achieve my purpose.'

My friend Lis Ainsworth had given me a book called *How to Multiply Your Baby's Intelligence* by the legendary brain developmentalist Glenn Doman. The book led me towards playing a proactive role in parenting, with an emphasis on giving my child a joyful learning experience. I did a complete turnaround. No more dentistry for me. I stayed home with Jett – and enjoyed it thoroughly. I pursued further education in Philadelphia and Sydney on early learning development, the human potential movement as it related to parenthood, and practical cognitive behavioural psychology (in the form of neuro-linguistic programming and neurosemantics) as it related to the human race.

The birth of Jett, and subsequently of Xian, gave me the reason (or was it an excuse?) to step away from dentistry and pursue something I truly love – and that is to give another human being the space to reach his or her highest potential and purpose. In so doing, I realised I wanted to actualise my own potential in what I was passionate about.

Through extensive coaching, mentoring and the learning partnership with my family, I learned how to boost and develop my self-awareness in order to become a better parent, professional facilitator, adult educator/trainer, speaker and transformational leadership coach. This is what I am doing still, and enjoying every minute of it!

Don't miss out on the present

Too often, you live for a future that has not yet arrived and reflect on a past that has gone by, only to miss out on the present, the here and now. You fail to recognise that being in the now has to be the most precious present you can give yourself – it is only in the now that you can really live and change anything you want.

It is about knowing what you truly want. Are you putting plans in place so that you have time to live in the moment – not in the past or future? By making conscious decisions to live for the present, you may gradually find yourself steering towards, if you will, a utopian state of mind.

*

Basically, are you living your purpose and 'pass-I-on' (passion is to pass yourself on in your endeavours) in the present? Are you doing what you love? Are you who you really want to be?

If you are, congratulations! If not, perhaps it may be time to take charge of yourself. Would you prefer to stop allowing things to 'happen' to you? As I found out, even your body can give you what you want when your mind contains a frequent and consistent (albeit, mostly unconscious) thought pattern. Articulate this clearly and regularly in your mind (sounds like a prayer, doesn't it?) – and you could get exactly what you want.

Are there any rules you need to change to do what you love? Go make your vocation your vacation. Mind your language to change the rules. Communicate the changes in your body so you can actualise what you would truly love to be. Self-coach by all means. Or get a professional coach to fast-track you. You'll never know if you never go. Make it your personal experiment to prove whether you can indeed change unconscious rules through changing your language, your mind and your bodily experiences.

The experiment: what if life is easy?

I am sitting in the mild winter midday sun overlooking Sydney Harbour tapping on my laptop. I am sipping a cappuccino and nibbling on a hazelnut torte smothered with rich dark chocolate – heavenly indulgence! The kids are still at school and I imbibe the freedom of having time just for me as I drink in the balmy sea air, listening to the boats lazily tinkling against their moorings, watching the overfed seagulls drift and glide overhead upon soft invisible breezes.

Life is good! Life is easy!

In the past, I would have feared being visited by demons and dragons breathing their fiery wrath upon me for daring to tempt fate with such a statement. Such a belief stems from my grandmother's legacy of ancient Chinese myths handed down to us as children – myriad tales of the tragedies befalling those who dared to be boastful of their good fortune.

That brings me back to conversations that were provoked by Philippa Bond, an inspiring educator and speaker, and Peter Spann, a self-made entrepreneurial millionaire and author of *Wealth Magic*. Based on their research and modelling of the ultra-wealthy from around the world, they suggest that the 'millionaire mindset' essentially comes down to three universal rules:

Life is easy.
Money is free.
You have a purpose.

Now, doesn't that go against practically everything you have been told since day dot? Well, maybe not the one about having a purpose. But the first two? If it were that simple, why are you not swimming in abundant riches? Why are you not overflowing with wealth beyond your imagination? Why are you all struggling to make it?

My circle of family, friends, colleagues and I must be duped! We have been indoctrinated to believe these rules:

Life is bitter.
Suffer for your art – or else it's not worth it.
Honest living comes from good hard work.
We work to live, we live to work.
Easy come, easy go.
It's too good to be true.
Money does not grow on trees.

Bond and Spann suggest that the amassing of wealth has much to do with the rules you live by. If your reality is to believe life is hard and money in short supply, evidence justifying that in your lives validates the rule. Each event then reinforces your belief that it is so – and you make decisions according to that reality. To change your reality, you must change the rules you live by.

Neuro-linguistic programming (NLP), according to the co-founders Richard Bandler and John Grinder, presupposes that 'if it is possible in the world, then it is possible for me – it is just a matter of how'. According to the NLP modelling study of present-day billionaires by Philippa Bond, successful modern entrepreneurs live by rules that can be replicated by all of us. Change the rules and change your life. Seems easy enough – it is just a matter of how.

Nature works in the following way. The bee goes for the nectar on the flower and, in the process, pollen gets rubbed off onto its legs. As the bee moves from blossom to blossom in its quest for sweet stuff, pollination occurs – a necessary byproduct for the reproduction cycle of the plant. Life is easy! So, why don't we humans (seemingly more evolved creatures than bees) just go for the nectar in our lives, and in the process leave a productive legacy as a consequence of our journey? Perhaps by instinct the bees live by the rule of 'going for the sweet stuff' and our neocortex has unwisely gone counterintuitive.

History tells us it is possible. About five hundred years ago, the artists of the Renaissance era produced works of art and architecture that continue to inspire us right up to this day. How was that possible? The Medici family, wealthy bankers from Florence, and their net-work of ultra-rich friends and colleagues decided to commission art intended to enrich and glorify the city-state of Florence and they became patrons to the likes of Leonardo da Vinci, Michelangelo and Raphael – thus ensuring that the artists could focus on fulfilling their passions and intentions: to freely paint, sculpt and design inspiring pieces as a legacy to humanity. So for these masters on (artistic) purpose: life was easy and money was free!

I am not suggesting that you suddenly ditch your job in order to fulfil your desire to paint half-clad exotic beauties on tropical isles (à la Gauguin) backed by the likes of Bill Gates, Richard Branson or Rupert Murdoch, or survive on alms offered by the community (unless you intend to don the saffron robes of Buddhist monks).

If it is possible in the world, it is possible for you – it is a matter of how. Okay. Let us assume that life is easy, money is free and you are on purpose. How will you live your life then? Will your belief in a true purpose inspire the universe to deliver that which you aspire to? Heaven knows – what is your purpose anyway? That is the question most of us find impossible to answer. It is in the genre of the meaning-of-life type discussions.

Perhaps it is also a matter of interpretation. Here's my reality check. I tossed and turned in my bed one night, nursing a very congested sinus and painful joints from the remnants of a viral flu that the kids had brought home. In the next room, my son slept restlessly with a plantar wart that obstinately continued to cling to his left foot for months. His sister absently scratched her head in her slumber, a reminder of an anti-lice hair treatment. Ah! The joys of winter ails . . . Is life really easy?

On the other hand, I felt totally guilty that that was all I had to complain about.

Come to think of it – something must have changed over time at the unconscious level. You see, deep down I do believe that for me life is easy, that money is free and I am happy living my purpose of being who I want to be right now.

Life is easy . . . compared with what? As of now, I joyously create and hold the space for my husband and children as we mutually share our life's experiences together – playing, working and growing in a learning partnership. Two beautiful kids (healthy except for the above complaints) and a supportive husband and co-parent – all three put up with my constant rantings and what they call my HLW ('high-level weirdness'). We live in a beautiful, warm and comfortable home in one of the most relaxed cities in the world. Food is fresh and plentiful. We enjoy clean water and healthy living. I have conveniences that make household administration seem more like being in robotics management – everything at the push of a button. I work with people I enjoy collaborating with, doing what I love.

Money is free . . . well, it seemed so for a while. Then I chose to be an 'opt-out mum' – you know, the high-achieving career woman type who walks out of a full-time job with pay and benefits 'to die for' to mostly stay home with the kids. But what is money? Is it fair to say it is a form of energy? Like all forms of energy, it can change or manifest itself in many ways. Also, it cannot be created or destroyed. It is neither good nor bad – it just is. It is the emotions you attach to it that cause your reactions to it. So, go on. Just tap into money for its potential usefulness (or not) to you.

You have a purpose. I consider myself a lucky person. I have been told that luck happens when opportunity meets preparedness. 'Lucky' could mean days of feeling snowed under with choices, when I can truly embrace that idiom of 'less is more'. Through the myriad choices that have passed my way, I have learned to say 'no'. This helps me focus on those opportunities I wish to pursue with purpose. Being on purpose gives me sovereignty over my life. I take a deep breath, step back and I reflect. What do I truly wish to do right now? Where do I want to be? With whom?

These are the times when I give myself permission to put everything aside. Watch my children play in the park. See the wonder of the world through new eyes. Look past the chaos and see the beauty of creation in the world. I am always rejuvenated after just a mere hour of that. And everybody – me, the children, our pet dogs and sometimes a few neighbours' kids – comes away happy. I am then ready to tackle anything.

In the western culture in which I have lived for most of my life, it seems you are encouraged to think that you have to 'do' things to get more from life. Yet, embracing my eastern genealogy, I believe that you can just 'be' who you are and that you will 'have' all you need. You just need to remember that.

And remember the saying: 'Be careful what you wish for – you may just get your wish.' So be specific about what you want. Otherwise it may arrive in a form you do not want. My colleague Bill often said, 'I wish I did not have to do this job anymore,' and he ended up with a serious disease that resulted in him leaving his job.

I am truly inspired by Mother Nature. I take her example – consciously going for the sweet stuff these days – and continue to be amazed by the surprising contributions I effortlessly add value to along the way. Go for the sweet stuff – and surprise yourself too!

Imagine what it would be like to believe that life is easy – and think about what that would mean to you. Step back and realise what it would be like for you if money were free. Have a sense of what it would be like to know that you have a purpose and are living your life exactly as you should be.

How would that be for you?

Applying the three Rs of partnering skills

In order for both learning partners – parent and child – to understand unconscious rules that can drive one another's behaviour, you can use these skills to prepare for the changing of rules:

1. *Reading* the rules: first, it is important to use the ARC process to identify what rule is driving the behaviour and whether it is useful or limiting.
2. *Righting*: next, when you discover that the unconscious rule is empowering you, consciously decide to use more of it – because it is 'right' for you.
3. *Re-writing*: when you realise an unconscious rule is limiting, choose to re-write it through the ARC process, re-patterning a more resourceful rule.

So which of these unconscious rules have you ruled out for you and your tribe because they hold you back from more expansive and satisfying experiences? What would it be like for you and your tribe to explore the ARC or re-patterning and surprise yourselves with what you discover?

Dos and don'ts

Do ask children lots of questions in a lovingly curious way

You may learn something from your kids. It is often difficult for a parent to know how much help children need, or how much should be given, as they gradually move to independence. Patience and always asking directed questions (rather than giving answers) are important strategies. Each time a child is successful in learning from within, his or her self-confidence or 'inner spirit' grows. The child will be willing to initiate learning again.

The quickest students are not those who are 'pushed' but the ones who set their own pace. This pace is determined by their 'inner spirit' and sense of competence. If children are to develop to their full potential, allow them to experience the joy of self-initiated learning – and experience your own delight.

Do pay it forward

Expect nothing in return. You care for your kids not just to expect the ROI (return on investment) of them caring for you in the future, but so that they may look after their children in the same manner or better – and for their kids to pay it forward . . . and so it goes on.

Don't make rules without assessing them meaningfully
You need to see if they work in your situation. A lot of rules are handed down because they are the ones you have experienced during your own upbringing. All meaning is contextual: if the rules fit, then try them on. Engage and explain to your children how they work and why. Get their buy-in.

Don't impose your perspective
Get the viewpoint of your children, especially when you encounter resistance to implementing any rules. You may learn something.

Personal learning journal

What rules do you observe with your children?

1.

2.

3.

4.

RULES

What other rules would you like to observe with your children?

1.

2.

3.

4.

Write down at least one thing you will implement immediately.

1.

SEVEN

Routine

Rules can help you and your tribe get into a routine. Are there rules that create useful boundaries in your schedule? What rules do you and your family keep to maintain a routine?

Some of us love routines, others loathe the thought of them. Regardless, the question to ask is: What would you do *without* routines?

Imagine a day without routines. There is the spontaneity of choosing to do whatever, whenever you want in the moment – great scope to experiment with new ideas about doing seemingly humdrum things. What would it be like brushing your teeth at work, rather than before you leave home? It could become a bit chaotic if there was no bus schedule or train timetable, and you had to wait until the appropriate ride appears. Imagine if the children woke up at random and made their own breakfast. Or if Mum, who previously consistently stocked the cupboard every Sunday afternoon, was experimenting with going to the store only when the children tell her what they want. And so it goes on.

Whether you like it or not, your lives are governed by routine – some minimal, others fleshed out in detail.

Why do you have a routine?

Routines promote trust

One of the simple benefits is that routines foster independence – and, in its turn, independence cultivates self-esteem and trust. Routines demonstrate a reliability that certain things will run at a certain time, and certain people will be in attendance when expected. Because of routines, there is less need to communicate about events that are slotted into a predetermined sequence, so people will show up at the appropriate times without being reminded.

Like consistent rules, nothing beats a regular routine so you do not need to occupy your mind trying to constantly re-invent how you do things. It allows for freedom from having to check with a supervisor all the time. Let's say you change meal times willy-nilly with a small child – that would be very confusing because the child would not know how much to eat. If he eats too much and is fed sooner than expected, he experiences force-feeding. If he does not consume enough and the next meal comes far later than it should, you will have a whiny, grumpy, hungry child. This is exacerbated when the child is too young to verbalise or signal his or her needs other than by crying and whimpering.

My children know their routines and they don't have to consult me all the time. They each have a timetable for their daily activities, which gives them the independence to prepare for their school day or activities without looking to me. Structured routine gives predictability and empowerment to act without constantly checking with parents. Jett and Xian know that their routine is to finish daily homework and music practice before watching television or playing computer games. So they know they don't have to ask for permission to play once they have completed their duties.

Routines kindle innovation

Routines free your creativity to improve. If you are not thinking of every step of your daily life, it allows you the liberty to explore and focus specifically on one thing at a time to learn, develop or improve. For example, if children know where their favourite book is all the time and can get back to it whenever they want, they are more likely to look for other books or activities secure in that knowledge.

Routines sustain role-modelling

As a role model, do you have a routine for yourself? Do you make 'me' time – the so-called 'self-spa' – by scheduling two or three gym workouts per week, setting a regular time to check emails or watching the evening news without interruption? If your children see that you have a routine, they will learn to respect your time too. It is preferable to co-create a structure in engaging clear boundaries to meet the needs of everyone affected. Routines can be changed through re-negotiation and partnering. For example, Ken or I take the children to school en route to work. But from time to time both of us are unable, so we have negotiated with the children that they take public transport on those days.

Routines are best worked out together

Initially, parents set the framework. But no matter how young the children, it is respectful to let them know why a certain routine is good for all. For example, regular sleep times help parents and children get into healthy recharging regimens so they can make the most out of their awake times without getting cranky.

Getting into the habit of creating relevance early on also demonstrates the importance of spelling out a reason in order to excite or motivate someone. When children are able to express themselves, it is useful to get them, as learning partners, to explain what good reasons they have in opposing the routine you are suggesting. Many a time, I have been inspired by their perspective. What's more, sometimes they have come up with a better routine than the one I proposed.

How does it work?

There are obvious daily routines for weekdays, weekends, holidays – ones that occur regularly.

An example of a weekday family routine when Jett was six and Xian four:

0645 Household wakes / toilet routines (brush teeth, shower, style hair, etc)
0730 Breakfast for all / pack lunches
0800 Depart for school, preschool or work
1200 Pick up Xian from preschool
1300 Lunch with Xian
1400 Afternoon siesta for Xian
1500 Pick up Jett from school
1530 Afternoon tea
1600 Violin or piano lesson
1730 Homework / music practice / cook dinner
1800 Ken comes home
1830 Dinner for all
1930 Clean up / Xian has bath / television or games
2000 Bedtime for Xian

2030 Get ready for bedtime (brush teeth, shower, pack school bag, read stories)
2100 Bedtime for Jett / lights out
2115 Parents' free time (reading / movies / television / chat)
2300 Bedtime for parents

Naturally, routines are likely to be more relaxed on weekends and holidays. Perhaps a 'no routine' holiday routine may in fact be a routine of spontaneity. Usually during the school holidays, we don't plan beyond the travel and accommodation. When we arrive at our destination, we play it by ear. It gives the children a chance to enjoy flexibility.

How do *you* deal with routine for yourself? Who have you involved in its creation? This is important when you are not particularly good with routines yourself. What routine or systems have you put in place that currently support you, your life and that of your family? By all means, do more of that! What routines are not working? Perhaps you can get inventive and re-design them to make them work better for you.

A word of caution. Beware of 'doing it right' – that is believing there is only one way, the so-called 'right way' to do things. There is much to be said for having options and flexibility to change things when necessity dictates. Routines are fine, provided there is room for continuous improvement, small tweaks that allow the system to develop and adapt to changing needs and environment.

Creativity can also be incorporated into the routine. Can you get creative with your routine (or with anything for that matter) when you need to?

The routine of creativity

Even creativity has a structure. How often have you started off with many bright ideas, only to watch them fizzle to nothing? What is the difference between those fertile ideas that successfully germinated into physical manifestation and the ones that merely began as great ideas and remained so?

What is creative intelligence?

Intelligence has been defined as the ability to recognise fine distinctions in a very specific area. It has been said that what is generally termed 'snow' can be categorised into a lexicon of more than twenty definitions by the Eskimo. Similarly, an oral microbiologist would probably be able to distinguish between thousands of microorganisms that exist in the ecosystem, compared with the one or two recognised by a layperson.

Walt Disney is widely accepted as a creative genius. His ability to connect innovative creativity with a successful business strategy and popular appeal allowed him to establish an empire in the field of entertainment that has survived decades after his death. Disney embodied the ability to make a successful organisation based on creativity. He represents the process of turning fantasies into concrete and tangible expressions, the ability to take something that exists only in the imagination and forge it into a physical existence that directly influences the experience of others in a positive way.

The structure of creativity

In the 1980s, Robert Dilts wrote a three-volume work entitled *Strategies of Genius* mapping the successful thinking strategies of people with special talents such as Walt Disney. Dilts worked out that Disney harvested his creative intelligence through a simple three-step process, which Dilts termed the 'three phases of creativity'.

Creativity involves the coordination of three processes: dreamer, realist and critic. A dreamer who is not a realist cannot turn ideas into tangible expressions. The processes of critic and a dreamer without the realist element may become stuck in a perpetual conflict. A dreamer/realist may create things, but might not achieve a high degree of quality without the critical process.

The point is that creativity itself involves the synthesis of different processes or phases. The dreamer is necessary for creativity in order to form new ideas and goals, the realist is necessary as a means to transform ideas into concrete expressions, and the critic is necessary as a filter helping to evaluate and refine the products of creativity.

Applying the creativity strategy

So what has Disney got to do with leadership, you might ask? Simply, by following the steps of his creative genius, your ideas and dreams for yourself and your tribe can come true.

Everybody already has the dreamer, realist and critic inside them. If you observe children, they naturally go through the Disney creative cycle: dream big first, get real next, then leave it up to Mum and/or Dad to criticise. Unfortunately, what typically happens in the adult is that the dreamer and critic get into a fight. Imagine there is a business meeting happening inside your head. Rather than following some organised strategy, the dreamer says something and the critic naturally argues against it. Then they both have a polarity reaction to each other, going in conflicting directions until finally the realist says, 'We're out of time.' Hence, chaos ensues and nothing happens.

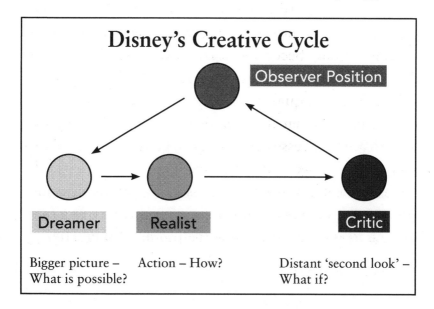

Disney's Creative Cycle

Observer Position

Dreamer — Realist — Critic

Bigger picture – What is possible? Action – How? Distant 'second look' – What if?

It is important to structure the relationship between these stages of creativity so it creates a harmonious process. The key is to acknowledge each thing will have multiple perspectives. The plan is to see all points of view – one at a time.

Let's imagine you are a manager who has gone on a professional development course and returned with new ideas galore. (I use a business example instead of a family example here because it is usually easier to harness the process naturally in children, whereas this tends to be counterintuitive in business.)

Dreamer

We know that Disney had a 'vision space' for the dreamer in which he allowed his body to relax into a dream state. In fact, he had a special room that was set up to be totally conducive to the dreamer: it had pictures and inspirational drawings and sayings all over the walls. Everything was chaotic and colourful in this room.

Create a space to permit the dreamer in you to come through. It may be a comfortable chair in a quiet room, or it could be a quiet park bench, or just closing your eyes and remembering a time when you were relaxed and able to creatively dream up new ideas without any inhibitions.

Disney believed his environment supported his inner self. He designed his dreamer room so that anything was possible there. There were soft cushions on the floor to lounge in, but no table and chairs. There were lots of crayons, paints and colouring pens, and a music system. Disney created a space where he and his team could create. He made that space so dreaming was easy. Not stiffly sitting down at a desk. He would lie on cushions on the floor, look up, roll around and allow the ideas to grow. He would not let any reality or criticism into the room.

When was the last time you created a space for yourself to dream? How many of you still dream? Do you think you have stopped dreaming? Or do you have more nightmares than dreams?

Children dream. Why don't we emulate children more? I encourage senior executives I coach to look not just at their team members, but at their family members at home. If they have lost their creative juices, I suggest they try finding them through observing their children. When was the last time you spent time with children to find out how to remain curious and excited about the wonderment of the world?

Once you are comfortable, run through all the ideas you have gleaned from the course and pick an outcome you want to achieve. While in this space, allow your creativity to really let loose. Visualise yourself accomplishing this goal as if you were a character in a movie. Imagine the changes in your environment as if they are in place already: new systems implemented, a fully contributing team who are completely satisfied, going beyond key performance indicators, fulfilling stakeholders' needs, and so on. Do not censor anything at this stage. Embellish and expand with great flourish. Have an attitude that anything is possible. In the dreamer state think 'big picture' – into the long-term future.

Realist

Disney set up an entirely different space for the realist to come through. Here, his animators had their own drawing tables, stocked with all kinds of modern equipment, tools and instruments that they needed to manifest the dreams. Tables were arranged in a large room in which all of the animators could see and talk to each other.

Disney's process of 'realising' his dreams took place by his literally stepping into the characters and viewing the dream-world through their eyes and through the 'storyboarding' process of splitting the dream into pieces. The realist acts as if the dream is possible and focuses on the formulation of a series of successive approximations of actions required to reach the dream.

In the realist room, Disney had state-of-the-art gadgets of his industry that could make his dreams come true. In your present world, that could be anything that involved computers and printers, recording equipment, measuring instruments, drafting boards, pencils and paper, ergonomic chairs and tables – whatever it takes to make your dream a reality. Once Disney had a dream, he would ask, 'Based on what I have now, what can I create in this room?' If he didn't have what he needed, he could source it out. In this room he might consult with experts who could help him. Even if he did not have the skills or resources, he could borrow, hire or engage in whatever form was useful to make the dream real. For instance, it was in this room (literally or metaphorically) where he talked to banks about what he wanted to achieve. Disney persevered by talking to over two hundred financial institutions to help make his dream come true.

Step into a different location from where you were as the dreamer. Perhaps you may be sitting upright in a straight-backed chair with your feet firmly planted on the floor. Maybe it helps to identify with a time when you were able to think realistically and have a sense of what that feels like.

Now associate into the 'dream' and feel yourself in the positions of all the relevant characters: the operations implementation team, the customer-facing frontline team, the board you report to, the customers, the shareholders, you. Then see the process as a sequence of images – that is, as a 'storyboard'.

Focus on 'how' to implement the plan or idea: the perfect performance management system, how you achieve extraordinary interpersonal relationships, a highly efficient communications system throughout the organisation, well-researched business development process, and so on.

The realist phase is more action with respect to the future and operates within a shorter time-frame than the dreamer phase.

Critic

For the critic, Disney had a little room that was underneath the stairs where his team would look at prototypes and pencil sketches and evaluate them. Because the room always seemed cramped and hot, it was called the 'sweatbox'.

Disney's process of critical evaluation involved separating himself from the project and taking a more distant 'second look' from the point of view of his audience or customers. The primary level of focus was on the 'why' of the plan. The critic seeks to avoid problems and ensure quality by logically applying different levels of criteria and checking how the idea or plan holds up under various 'what if' scenarios.

The critic phase involves analysing the plan in order to find out what could go wrong and how that could be avoided. It means considering both long- and short-term issues, searching for potential sources of problems in both the past and the future.

The critic room is where Disney invited constructive feedback and judgement of the work or vision before it got out to the audience or consumer. This is where quality control happens. Look at your work or vision and ask: Why wouldn't people buy that dream? Why am I not getting funding from venture capitalists? Why are my clients not wanting this? This is about stepping back, taking control and looking to see how you can make it better.

Create another space far enough away from the dreamer and the realist to prevent the critic interfering with them, and vice versa. Remember, the critic is there to criticise the plan, *not the realist or the dreamer. It is often helpful for the critic to identify which elements of the plan are satisfactory before asking questions. Now think of anything that may be missing or needed to real- ise the dream. Turn the criticisms into 'how' questions for the dreamer: How do I get the resources to implement these steps? Do I need to read more books or attend yet another professional development course? Or get profes- sional advice or find a mentor? Change industry?*

Step back into the dreamer and realist positions to come up with solutions, alternatives and additions to address the questions posed by the critic.

Observer

If the critic's questions seem too harsh or it is difficult to think of any questions without accessing the critic state, step into a neutral observer position away from the dreamer, realist and critic. You may even wish to rephrase the critic's questions from this observer position.

You need to step back. Disney stood back from his three rooms on the observer level to check for gaps, for what might have been missing and what still needed to be integrated to make his vision happen. For example, do you need more finance? Do you need other expertise to make this happen? Do you need resources and technolo- gies that have not been accounted for? Is the tone/theme/ colour of the project consistent throughout? Do you need more contrast? What is the next step?

*

And then, take the first step. Often ideas happening in your head never make it into the world. How are you to manifest your vision if these ideas remain unexpressed?

Managing creativity in a team

One powerful form of team learning and creativity arises out of the fact that people have different 'maps' of the world. Applying Disney's strategies takes advantage of this natural process of team learning and co-creativity, which is called 'inter-vision'. In 'supervision' there is an implied hierarchical relationship between people; the supervisor provides the 'right map' to the other person. In 'inter-vision' it is assumed that people are peers and that there is no one right map.

The creative cycle of a team often revolves around the relationship between 'the big picture' and the short-term objectives required to reach the overall goal. A key part of managing the group's creativity involves the ability to break down the general roles of the team members into specific, cognitive and interactive processes. The exercise is thus organised into the three phases of dreamer, realist and critic.

Dreamer
One of the group members, let's call her the 'explorer', describes a plan or idea to the other members. The idea may be to install a new rewards incentive system in the team.

The group members focus on widening, enriching and clarifying their mental perception of the idea by such questions as:

- What do you want to do?
- Why do you want to do it?
- What is the purpose?
- What are the payoffs?
- How will you know when you have achieved them?
- When can you expect to achieve them?
- Where do you want the idea to take you in the future?
- Who do you want to be or be like in relationship to the idea?

Realist

Each group member (including the explorer) is to make a simple storyboard of the plan or idea. Act as if the dream is achievable and consider how the idea or plan can be implemented. Identify specific actions and define the steps towards achieving short-term goals. Each member must put him or herself in the shoes of all the people involved in the plan and perceive it from those different points of view: sales manager, sales team members, marketing team members, channel partners, customers, industry peers, suppliers, shareholders, board members, the community at large, and so on.

The following realist questions can be explored:

- What are the specifics of the way the idea would be implemented?
- How will you know if the goal is achieved?
- How will the performance criteria be tested?
- Who will do it? (Assign responsibility and secure commitment from those carrying out the plan.)
- When will each phase be implemented?
- When will the overall goal be completed?
- Where will each phase be carried out?
- Why is each step necessary?

Critic

The separate storyboards are synthesised into a common storyboard. This is typically done by the explorer while restating the plan or idea.

The group then takes a 'second look' at this new combined storyboard, preferably by physically changing location to get an effective distancing from the previous two stages. The purpose is to help avoid problems by taking different perspectives and finding missing links by logically identifying potential problems and considering what would happen if these occur.

In order to be constructive, the group members can first acknowledge which criteria have been met, and formulate their criticisms into questions as much as possible, for example:

- Does this plan match the criteria and purpose for which it was intended?

- For what reasons might someone object to this new idea?
- Who will this new idea affect?
- Who will make or break the effectiveness of the idea and what are their needs and payoffs?
- What are the positive elements in the current way(s) of doing things?
- How can those elements be kept when the new plan or idea is implemented?
- When and where would you not want to implement this idea?

So the next time a new idea is begging to materialise, remember to get into the Disney creative strategy, cycling from the dreamer and the realist to the critic until you arrive at the version of the plan that is congruent with the outcome you desire to achieve.

Sow the seeds of your desired outcome on prepared and fertilised soil. Allow them to germinate, grow and blossom. Weed and prune as necessary to help them thrive. Trust that you now have what it takes to creatively implement new ideas and plans.

Getting creative with routines

Now that you have the structure of creativity to model, how can you apply this to your routines?

Let's say you want to re-engineer a new weekday routine in the new year. School timetables have changed, work commitments have altered, extracurricular and lei-sure activities for all of you have been re-arranged. How can you make it work for the whole family?

Putting aside a couple of hours, you may choose to facilitate the following:

1. *Dreamer*: Get into a space where you all can imag-ine an ideal weekday when your life is running smoothly and beautifully. What will it look like from start to finish? Brainstorm it with images, tone, emotions, activities, smells, music – together. Get everyone involved. Do not edit anything. Create a poster or mind-map that can be put up somewhere so the whole family can see it and keep this dream alive.

2. *Realist*: Make a spreadsheet of each family mem-ber's schedules to fit into the routine. Use Post-its to drop items into the weekday template – classify them as 'must-do', 'nice-to-do' and 'love-to-do'. Get everyone involved.

3. *Critic*: One person can now present the draft rou-tine to the whole family. The rest of the family can look for ways to improve it. For instance, is there flexibility in the routine? Are there any exceptions you need to consider in the daily routine? What is the charter of agreement among the family mem-bers about holding everyone accountable to this. What will bring you to review the routine?

*

Reviewing the example above, can you think of other ways of using the Disney creative cycle with the family in re-creating routines? Are there any other contexts for using this pattern? How can you use this with other tribes?

Applying the three Rs of partnering skills

Once again, you can choose to use these skills to assess whether the current routine is working or needs tweaking:

1. *Reading*: Step back and look at the current facts – what is working and what could be further developed?
2. *Righting*: Acknowledge what is working in the routine.
3. *Re-writing*: If the routine could be improved, make the necessary changes, making sure you involve those affected in the redevelopment.

So what routines are in place to support you, your life and that of your family? By all means, do more of that. What isn't? Perhaps you can get creative and re-design the routine to make it work better for you.

Dos and don'ts

Do reproduce these learning partnerships at will and with regularity

Start with *intention*, then *awareness*. It can be clumsy at first but, like anything, the more you do, the easier it gets.

Do routinely celebrate confusion, discomfort, awkwardness

Why? Because if you are feeling entirely familiar and at ease, then you are *not learning* anything new. They are what learning partnerships can feel – and the *rewards* of stretching your comfort zone means that these initially uncomfortable boundaries will become comfortable over time. Children simply do this better than adults. Model them. Have you ever seen a baby fall down three times and give up – never to walk again? Walt Disney approached hundreds of financiers to help him make Mickey Mouse a reality – it took the last institution to say yes or else we would not have Disney theme parks and movies today.

Don't be perfect

Be magnificently imperfect.

Personal learning journal

Write down how you deal with routine.

ROUTINE

1.

2.

3.

4.

Write down the thoughts and feelings you had from this lesson.

1.

2.

3.

4.

Write down at least one thing you will implement immediately.

1.

EIGHT

Review and Reflect

Now let's consider the process involved in making a routine of constantly improving your lives. Do you make time to pause in your busyness? Do you make time to pause to review and reflect?

R&R is the abbreviation for 'rest and relaxation' popularised by the war movies of the 1950s when GIs went on leave. The meaning of R&R here is also about taking a break from the routine. It is your ability to pause, take stock of what's working or not, celebrate the wins, sharpen your axe and challenge yourself to new ways of doing better.

Reviewing and reflecting means to 'practise the pause'. I have chosen to call this the 'R&R' for the family. This R&R could be personal, or it could involve the whole family at once.

R&R is as important, if not more so, as the 'doing' to realise your vision through your actions.

R&R is another avenue that allows learning partnerships to thrive. Taking time out regularly with the family (and your own self) to reflect and review provides opportunities to improve, develop and evolve yourself. A charter of agreement here could be useful: that during R&R, every win – no matter how small – is worth celebrating, any idea – no matter how seemingly trivial – is worth considering.

R&R could be part of your routine – annually (such as through a New Year's resolution), quarterly, monthly, weekly or even as often as daily.

How does it work?

Here's an example of a simple R&R process to use when conducting your family meetings:

1. *What's hurting?* Review what is not working and brainstorm suggestions about how to do things differently. Be grateful for the opportunity to do better. Indeed, count your blessings.
2. *What's working?* Too often we forget to count – and in fact discount – what we consider 'only small wins'. Do you remember how, in kindergarten and primary school, the teachers make small but constant awards to the children? It is the

validation that positively reinforces the behaviour you want developed – frequently, simply and joyfully. Celebrating often is key. Indeed, count your bliss.

So who is accountable for keeping you to the R&R? Let me suggest that it could be part of the family charter. The parents should certainly start the process off. But it is most effective when all members facilitate this process. On an individual basis, the buck then stops with you.

When I was growing up, an annual gathering of the family at Chinese New Year created a natural opportunity for my father to initiate the process for the year. We had family meetings and one of the four daughters took the minutes. We rotated as the 'keeper of the minutes'. In the same manner, you could elect to have a member of the family be a facilitator for the R&R for the year and a different person the keeper of the R&R for a monthly, quarterly or annual period.

Should there be an extraordinary need to have an R&R meeting, it would only seem natural that whoever called for the R&R session would be the facilitator.

It is during our (scheduled or extraordinary) R&R sessions that we get conversational re-setting or re-negotiation of routines. The type of family meetings my father held were more formal versions where minutes were recorded and kept. However, currently the frequency of our communications, and the honesty and transparency we have to re-negotiate and co-create, have not made such formal meetings as necessary. Yet I do not see it as out of the question should it arise in the future: who knows what changes abound?

As simple as it sounds, this R&R process is too often under-utilised. The excuse is the usual: 'There is no time . . . we are too busy.' What is the point of existing just to be doing, doing, doing? Why not stop and simply be in bliss – no matter how fleeting this may be? What is the meaning of life? I propose that it is not a tangible endpoint or destination. It can easily be found in daily doses of small moments of joy in life's journey. Remembering to count these regularly is what gives life meaning.

How we have used R&R in our family

1. *Stepping away from an emotionally charged experience*, which is a common occurrence when being around loved ones. It allows you to take the charge out of extremely negative (and even positive) experiences that can blind you. I remember as a teenager what it was like to be yelled at to finish a school assignment rather than abandoning it to run off to a party. Instead of slamming the door on Mum as she's screaming out at us, what would it be like if we took the time to step back and look at the situation, then sat down and negotiated a 'time out' for relaxation so we can be more efficient in our project when we return to it (sketching

our intended timeline for completion of the project for her as we waltz out the door).

2. *Counting versus discounting*: It could be just a way of stepping back and counting (rather than discounting) all the things (no matter how miniscule) that you have achieved or won during the day. I remember nagging my son about letting his violin practice slide during the holidays. What I was obsessing about was the fact that he had been spending a lot of quality time with his younger sister, showing her the beauty of Game Boy. Look, I am not about to debate the benefits and disadvantages of music practice over those couch-potato-RSI-developing toys (you can tell where I stand). What I failed to take into account is the beautiful relationship he was building with his sibling.

3. *Celebrate*: Reviewing allows you to 'count' and celebrate all your wins (no matter how small). When the children were small every day was about reflecting on their first smile, first words, first steps. You need to continue to count the little steps and tweaks to 'leave things better than when we found them' – for example, one of the ways is when picking them up from school, or when I am tucking Jett and Xian up in bed, we talk about 'the best thing that happened today'. It's like going through the daily rushes of the movie of our lives – as a director. I then encourage them to celebrate and

161

remember so they can re-create more of these amazing moments.

4. *Learning opportunity*: Sure, there are times when things do not go as planned – and in fact are seemingly way off course. Reviewing and reflecting allows you to take stock of how you could have done better. I will ask the children, 'What did not go well today? How did it make you feel?' That allows them to archive these rushes from the cutting-room floor (not discard them, because they can be great lessons to refer back to) and I ask them to re-edit them so that if a similar situation happens again they will rehearse how they would like it to be, how they would like it to make them feel, and how they could make that happen. We even have a bit of fun playing the movie backwards with circus music and getting them to dissociate from it – getting a bit more laughter and creativity (there is a fine line between silliness and genius, right?) – and then re-writing the event and storing it for future reference.

Here is another take on R&R. Jim Loehr and Tony Schwartz, in their book *The Power of Full Engagement*, wrote about the need to step back regularly to review and reflect. They counselled that managing energy (not time) is a key to a great life of health and happiness. Doing so gives you time to recover in your very busy modern lives. This concept covers a role-modelling opportunity, a self-respecting routine, not to mention a rule change about 'recharging for resilience' instead of 'stress and time management'.

Don't take my word for it. Do go ahead. Practise the pause. What difference did it make for you? Will making regular time to review and reflect bring you more wisdom? Can you also find ways to review and reflect so that there is less conflict between you and your tribe?

Wisdom through multiple perspectives

Let me invite you to explore another process that can help dissolve and resolve conflicts.

'That car in front is dumb!' five-year-old Xian commented, as I was driving my brood to school one morning. My intuitive response was to give Xian my take on her comment: that cars are inanimate objects and that they cannot sense things like we do. She means the *driver* of the car is dumb, right? Instead, I had learned since I had had my first-born, Jett, that it is usually safer to go counterintuitive.

So instead I said, 'I am curious because I thought cars can't possibly be dumb because they don't feel or sense things like we do.' (I felt good about getting my opinion across this way.) 'What makes you think they can feel like that?'

'When cars collide,' Jett piped up, 'they sense the collision and their air bags come out as a result.' Sure, it does seem that cars can *react* to circumstances.

Xian continued, 'When you park your car, Mum, and get too close to something you could hit, the car tells you so by beeping.' Point taken – some cars have parking *sensors* (not quite like our five *senses*, but close).

Okay. I get it. Cars have sensors and seemingly can react predictably . . . and I can see the metaphorical equivalent.

The point is: if I had jumped in to state my view on the matter, I would have lost the opportunity to wander into my children's world and explore it from their perspective.

Acknowledging different worldviews

Isn't it fascinating how children think? Too often, I have been guilty of not listening and simply imposing my model of the world (or my Matrix – see chapter four) on them. I am now on a mission to navigate every one of the models by which my children perceive and construct their world or matrix. What amazes me most consistently are the insightful perspectives by which they experience the world.

As parents, you are given the gifts of your children, I believe, as a magical mirror by which they can honestly reflect what you most need to develop in yourselves. It is truly an unconditionally loving learning partnership. Your part is not to be too anxious about 'doing' parenting perfectly. It is about welcoming this natural collaboration in which, as you grow to your authentic best and uncover your innate genius, you allow their inborn genius to blossom, flourish and express itself.

Buckminster Fuller, the American philosopher and

architect, said, 'We are all born geniuses. It is society that de-geniuses us,' through the limiting beliefs that get installed unconsciously along the way.

As parents and caregivers holding the space for children to live their highest potential, it is an honour and privilege to be modelling genius at its best. It certainly makes parenting seem less of a necessary responsibility and more of a joyful experience of collaborative development.

Have you ever thought about how children find wonder in all that they see, hear and do?

What is it that makes children find new possibilities so easily?

What compels children to find learning fun and joyful?

When did you, in essence, stop being a child?

How can you rediscover the genius within you and allow this child prodigy to express itself?

What would it be like for you if parenting were simply a journey of stepping into the world of your children and making a conscious decision to review what you have learned to think and feel is true and consider other possibilities of reality?

Conversely, consider that you are the mirror through which your children look so you can reflect to them what they most need to learn.

What possibilities open up for you in the magnificent balance of this beautiful learning partnership?

Would parenting become less laborious and more joyful if you see this role as less of what you have to do and more of what you love to be?

The wisdom pattern for parenting

A wise person once told me, 'Your opinion is worth nothing . . . if that is all you have.' What does that mean?

Imagine yourself face to face with your children holding a pen horizontally in front of you. They say to you, 'The pen nib is pointing to the *left*.' From your vantage point, there is no doubt it is pointing *right*. Both answers are correct from your individual points of view. Yet the two statements are diametrically opposed. At that level of thinking, there is no agreement. If you then looked at it from a third perspective, one that makes the situation true for both parties, and say, 'The nib is pointing *north* [or whatever cardinal point of the compass is true at the time],' you would now be in agreement.

This is what is called 'wisdom', the ability to see one situation from multiple perspectives. In order to be wiser in any circumstance, you need to train yourself to experience an event from a minimum of three positions. This is what is called the *wisdom pattern*.

In any interpersonal interaction between parents and children, there is an assumption for a positive outcome: that you have an *intention* to get along, that you want to resolve any issue or at least to come through with an objective non-judgemental result.

My children and I have had a big day out together. Jett and Xian are fighting over what I consider a petty issue yet again, and I am losing it. They are screaming and pushing at each other. My attempts to separate them physically are falling on deaf ears. I raise my voice with stronger threats – to no avail. I am exhausted. If I do not do something quickly, somebody is going to get hurt. What do I do? My initial thoughts are to smack them both and send them to bed with no dinner. Should not a mother at the end of her tether be allowed to impose her authority because she can?

I take a deep breath and decide to step back instead and consider the wisdom pattern.

Moving through multiple perspectives

From my perspective, which I shall term the *first position*, I can say unreservedly that it takes two to get a fight going. As the children have heard me say time and again, it does not matter who started the fight. Whoever continues it is just as much in the wrong. 'Stop fighting and use your words' – that is, work out your differences yourselves – 'or you will both be punished.' This is what I yell over the din. Nobody is taking any notice. At this rate, I will have to punish them both. I do not believe in violence as a disciplinary option, and yet the thought of smacking them is surfacing quickly.

From the *second position* – where the children are coming from – they are not listening to my usual banter about both being in the wrong regardless of who initiated it. They've heard it all before. Somebody has to be *more* wrong, and Mum should just deal with the matter for us.

Can't she see that we can't work it out – whether with words or fisticuffs? She has to help us work this out – after all, isn't that what Mum should do? She fixes everything. Come on, Mum, tell us who is wrong: use *your* words. Then, to be fair, punish the culprit and get on with it.

Should we continue to maintain our respective positions, the situation is likely to get more heated and deteriorate further. The more we stick to our guns, the more emotional the conflict will be.

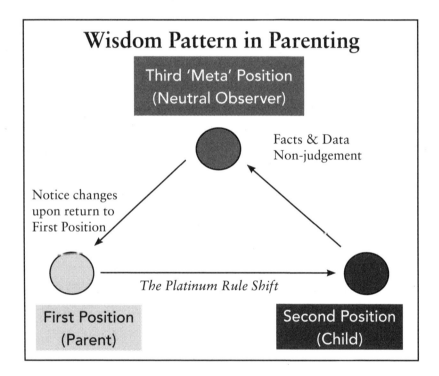

Wisdom Pattern in Parenting

Third 'Meta' Position
(Neutral Observer)

Facts & Data
Non-judgement

Notice changes
upon return to
First Position

The Platinum Rule Shift

First Position
(Parent)

Second Position
(Child)

The platinum rule of wisdom
Most people have heard of the golden rule of wisdom, which spans many cultures: 'Do unto others as *you*

would like *them* to do unto *you*.' Let me relate to you the rule that overrides it. The platinum rule of wisdom is: 'Do unto others as *they* would like *you* to do unto *them*.'

Imagine what it would be like if I step into the children's shoes and experience the whole situation through their points of view. As I go into the second position, I now see myself in the first position, in my angry mother role, and experience it as if I were the children. I begin to appreciate why the children were not listening because I truly did not understand where they were coming from. Here I was playing the authoritarian tyrant, getting frustrated trying to get myself heard over the din. Instead, it seems that it would be more useful if I use words to create a situation where each of the children can be heard.

What if I am a fly on the wall? As a neutral observer, I can see and hear a mother trying to stop a fight that is escalating between two children. The children are becoming more physically violent, and the mother is raising her voice higher and higher. The children are ignoring the mother. She clenches her jaw and fists and stands, seemingly contemplating what to do next. This is a factual and unemotional report from a third position.

From this 'meta' (meaning above and beyond the particular situation) perspective, there is no judgement. Because this third position forces me to step back and look at this 'movie' without the emotions, I now begin to see that it would not be possible to stop the fight by punishing both because resentment could still simmer if I, as the authority figure, simply told them to do so. It would be more useful to give each of them the opportunity to voice their case in a manner perceived as fair and equitable to both.

Now that I have looked at this matter from three different perspectives, I return to the first position and notice what has changed. I discover that the situation is now less charged and I can respond with more objectivity and calmness. I take a deep breath and stand between the children, saying firmly, 'I need your help. Please stop so we can all talk about what is happening *now*.'

Miraculously, Jett and Xian stop and look at me with enquiring eyes. I tell them that I am sad to see brother and sister fighting and I want them to help me see what has caused the situation so we can prevent it happening again. They both agree to help. I ask them to go to two separate rooms – where I spend just two minutes with each. I ask each to tell me what (not who) caused the fight and how they could prevent it from happening again.

From the mouths of babes

The following uncorroborated information surfaces.

Jett tells me that I do not get angry as easily as others (their dad, grandparents and teachers) so they feel comfortable fighting in my presence. I ask him if he knows that even though I do not express my anger to the same degree, I feel very sad and disappointed because I do not like violent behaviour. Shaking his head, he says he didn't know that. But now that he knows, he would help me by not baiting his sister as much. Instead, should she start the fight, he will remind her that Mum is happier if we try to work things out instead because Mum is saddened by violence.

Xian says that her brother brings out the worst in her when I am there and she feels comfortable trying to sort things out physically because I do not get angry easily. (There it is again.) When she finds out that I feel sadness and disappointment instead of anger, she also decides to help by using words instead of punches and kicks to resolve conflicts with Jett.

There have been minimal fights between the two children since our conversation. I am amazed at how children honour their words.

Isn't it interesting that, despite my abhorrence of violent behaviour, in a crisis my initial instinct was to resort to violence (smack the kids)? Would that have been a useful behaviour to model to the children if I had done it? In choosing to be counterintuitive, and to ask for the children's help, we resolved the problem by me inviting them to be part of the solution.

Have a go

Don't take my word for it. Try thinking it through yourself with situations that have occurred in the past (or which may be happening right now). For instance, it may be a disagreement with your significant other about the discipline of the children or an argument you have with your mother-in-law. Perhaps it is an angry exchange with your teenager over the completion (or not) of a task. Move through the three positions and notice what has changed when you return to first base.

When one is making future plans, wisdom training could be useful to research the different angles. The viewpoints of different stakeholders could be identified and worked through objectively. For instance, before planning a family holiday, it may be interesting to explore the perspectives of your spouse, the children or even the house- or dog-sitter about when you are away.

So the next time you are faced with a situation that could potentially turn ugly, I invite you to explore the wisdom pattern – it is a simple tool to defuse a highly charged situation and to gain new insights or possibilities in any interpersonal impasse.

Use it in other parts of your life

The skill of wisdom training can be applied to times when you are dealing with business associates, friends and social acquaintances. Pounce at the opportunity to turn around a potentially explosive argument with your business partner. What about those debates you have with your mates concerning, say, politics, sports and religion? And those dinner parties when a controversial topic is introduced and those present start to stake out their battle stations.

You will be amazed at how just one person altering

their response completely changes the dynamics of the situation. Once again, don't take my word for it. Go test it.

Rest assured that the more you learn and practise this wisdom pattern, the more you will realise the impact of parenting applications in all areas of your life. The more you are conscious of different perspectives occurring in different contexts from day to day, the more you will notice the transformation in your ideal way of being who you are when relating to colleagues, business associates, team members, clients, acquaintances, friends, family and all those meaningful people in your life.

After all, isn't parenting about being your authentic best so you can be a role model to unleash the highest potential in your children? Enjoy exploring the genius in you. Here's to the joy of parenthood and the gaining of parenting wisdom.

Applying the three Rs of partnering skills

Let's navigate these skills to assess what actually needs tweaking during R&R:

1. *Reading*: Step back into your R&R, and become aware of the current facts in the context you are reviewing.
2. *Righting*: Reflecting on what has been reviewed, celebrate what is right and great to continue.
3. *Re-writing*: Note the parts of the review that need

173

tweaking and reflect on what to stop, start or develop. This may include stepping through the wisdom pattern of multiple perspectives if there are some relationship conflicts to deal with. Then reframe and re-write the context to excite the tribe.

Reviewing and reflecting allows you to take stock of where you are at and steer towards where you wish to go. It's a checkpoint, a place where you realign, change course or celebrate being on track or better!

So have you planned your R&R to pause and celebrate or make small tweaks regularly?

Dos and don'ts

Do observe . . . to lead your children to thrive in a rapidly changing world

Help them understand that they have a choice to *lead* themselves out of any situation. They have five magnificent senses that, if engaged in heightened awareness, essentially create a sixth sense: the amazing ability to calibrate minute changes (what you *normally* cannot seem to perceive) and adjust to the situations immediately.

When kids are hyperactive they are labelled ADHD and medicated. Truly observe your children better and learn from them. Could it be that their so-called hyperactivity is an adaptation or evolution to your rapidly changing world?

Do expect great things of you and your children

What you expect of yourself tends to be reflected in your children – for example, if you had wanted to achieve better academic results than you did obtain, you may tend to push your children to achieve what you missed out in life. The vacuum in your life can drive you, and your kids, to distraction.

Learn more about yourself. Understand that your children are different. Notice this trigger: when you persist on being adamant about something and your children are taking the opposite opinion, be open to discussing different approaches with them. You may all want the same thing and the disagreement may simply be a difference about how to get there.

Suzuki pedagogy is based on the premise that all children have ability – not that all children will develop at the same rate but that, given good environmental conditions, their ability will be fostered. Your expectation of your children is part of this environment and an experiment in an American school proved this: children in one class performed exceptionally well for no other reason than the teacher thought they were bright. So, for the sake of your children, keep having faith in their ability, whatever the evidence to the contrary.

Eleanor Roosevelt could not read at the age of seven. At the same age, Albert Einstein's schoolteacher declared that the boy would not amount to anything. Winston Churchill failed his entry into military college. Each of these people went on to make significant contributions to the world.

Traditional education systems are, of necessity, concerned with children achieving in a particular time-frame. Working with your children at home allows them to learn at the right rate for them. So keep faith with your children's ability and foster it.

Expect your children to succeed and they will.

'Any child can develop in any way,' said Dr Suzuki.

Do celebrate joyful times in your life when you were learning from one another

In my travels around the world, and through blogs, tweeting, coaching conversations, I have been so fortunate to have shared with many parents the wonderful learnings from their children. Please feel free to visit my website (www.dryvonnesum.com) and blog (www.dryvonnesum. com/blog) to read the success stories. Or participate in the conversations on my Facebook page (www.facebook.com/DrYvonneSum), LinkedIn (www.linkedin.com/in/dryvonnesum) or Twitter (https://twitter.com/YvonneSum). Why not learn from *your* network so you may have even *more* learning partners in your life? In other words, why not start a playpals mastermind group?

Remember if you can set up simple ways of celebrating your own little achievements, it becomes natural for your children to do the same for themselves. You usually celebrate the artworks that your children bring home by putting them on the fridge or by congratulating their makers. Have you announced your ecstasy (or described the challenging learnings) in completing a project well (or not as well as you would like) and sharing it at the table with your family at dinner? By doing that constantly, and inviting all the members of your tribe to share their wins (and awareness of new learnings) of the day, they learn to proactively acknowledge their own progress and achievements rather than wait for external validation from others first.

Don't settle for mediocrity

Take time out to review and reflect: 'Is this the best we can do?' Remember Steve Jobs's legacy of the revolutionary spirit: let's challenge the status quo to put a ding in your universe to make your world a better place.

Personal learning journal

What have you achieved or won during the day (today or yesterday)?

1.

2.

3.

4.

What is at least one thing you would like to change immediately?

1.

Write down at least one thing you will implement immediately.

1.

NINE

Reorganise

When you have paused to 'think', when you have reviewed and reflected on that which needs doing or changing, the next step is to make it happen – putting the 'thinking' into 'doing' in a new way. It is to reorganise.

Reorganising is simply the 'doing' that naturally flows on from R&R 'thinking'. Based upon agreement about what is operating well or not, you can make the necessary adjustments: by 'doing' more of the things that are working through incorporating the new 'thinking' or more of the ideas that alleviate what was hurting.

It's good to set up rules for the children when they are toddlers – but won't the rules change when they are in their teens? Absolutely. So you need to reorganise. You review and reflect and then start reorganising what needs to be changed. Some rules will remain the same. Others will need to be added to or refashioned – for example, toilet training rules for two-year-olds will no longer apply when your children are ten!

When you realise that a belief (rule) is not useful, finding a way to reframe it may take a bit more effort. Case in point: nine-year-old Xian believed she could not travel on the bus to school without another adult. Up until then, we had caught buses together for other destinations except to school. We managed to reframe the rule by Xian travelling the route to school and back once with me and now she can do it on her own. In order to reorganise the rule to give Xian the opportunity of being independent in getting to and from school on her own (because neither Ken nor I could always take her, and we did not want to get someone else to accompany her), we made a plan for it to happen (see point 1 below). She now believes that she *can* do it, although she still prefers not to – why would you when you have been chauffeured by your parents up until you were nine years old? But this reorganisation needed quite a bit of effort!

It is well-nigh impossible to separate the description of reorganising the 'doing' of, say, a routine, from setting out what R&R 'thinking' went into it in the first place. To continue to 'leave things better than when we found them', you need to constantly reorganise. Sometimes this is a natural reordering of process. At other times, you have to put heaps more effort in.

Major redesign

Now and then, there may need to be whole system changes that can seem like a major revamp of routines. Some examples of reorganising in my family include:

1. *Ride to school.* Up until the children were in junior primary school, Ken and I had been taking them to school by car en route to work. As their independence and confidence grew, we trusted them to take public transport to and from school. We had an R&R with the kids to organise how to transition the travel to and from school by car to one by bus or train. Here were the steps:
   a. Mum takes the bus run with Xian and Jett together (to and from). Mum points out the train route along the way to Jett (who prefers taking the train).
   b. Jett waits with Xian at the bus stop to put her on bus before he gets on his train.
   c. Xian comes home by bus with a school friend. Jett comes home by train on his own.
   d. Xian catches the bus to and from school by herself.
2. *Mum returns to full-time work.* Mum used to work around the children's activities, whether it was school pick-ups and drop-offs or chauffeuring to ballet or tap classes, violin or piano lessons. When Mum got back to full-time work, which required a

reasonable amount of interstate and international travel, co-parents (who both need to travel in their roles) had an R&R to tweak how diaries could be synchronised ahead of time so at least one parent is always in town for the children.

3. *Changes in the civil code* – for example, any changes or additional criteria to the FGBP points system – will naturally mean that when they are revoked, it will be by the same amount and for the new conditions negotiated. (See 'Frequent good behaviour points' on page 92.)

Minor remodel

Most of the time, though, the rule changes can be small. They occur incrementally so that the shift by degrees seems imperceptible. It is very much like a niece or nephew who has gradually been growing taller – seemingly unnoticed by the parents until the aunt or uncle exclaims, 'How big you have grown!' at the annual family do.

From little things big things grow.

How does it work?

Two examples:

1. *Helping with household.* In recognition of the children's growing abilities, and their desire to

contribute to the family community, it is rewarding to be gradually giving them more and more responsibility. It shows respect, it encourages partnering, it is about making a routine that constantly gets R&R'd, updated and reorganised. Furthermore, it role-models advancing contributions to the family. This is what we have been doing progressively during our weekly grocery shopping routine: at two years of age, the kids helped us spot the items on the list as I called them out; at four, they started getting the items within their reach off the shelf; at six, they were given the responsibility of holding the list, reading items off it and checking them off; at eight, they helped me work out change at the check-out counter; at ten, they were each given a section of the list, collected the respective items and met us back at the check-out for payment. By the time they reached twelve they were getting the grocery shopping done and meeting me at another store where I was running other errands.

2. *Homework and music practice.* Children enjoy the trust and independence you afford them. Their self-esteem soars with what they perceive as ever more respect. This can be achieved with a gradual increase of responsibility for their own work.

   a. At six years of age, I initiate this self-perpetuating routine of reorganising, which incorporates R&R constantly along the way. Their duty was as timekeepers – we did no more

183

than ten-minute sections of homework or music practice daily. I sat close by to observe – only checking in to ask questions and direct them back when I noticed they were off track, without giving the answers.

b. At seven years of age, they proceeded as above except for this change: I assisted (again with directional questions) only when invited.

c. At eight, sessions were increased to twenty minutes, with me floating in and out of their working space.

d. At nine, as above, except they chose when to do their homework or music practice – I only checked in with a question about how it was going if I noticed none being done, and I would not sign their school homework or practice diary unless the work was sighted.

e. At ten, they showed me their work as they prompted me to sign their diary (they filled in details themselves). If they had not completed a project and needed an extension, I helped coach them in planning the request to their teacher (assisted with a signed note from me) but they needed to do the presentation themselves.

f. At twelve, I expected them to draft the note seeking special consideration for a project extension, which I was happy to countersign if the reason was satisfactory.

What are *you* doing to transform the R&R agreements into reorganised action plans in your family?

How often have you got stuck in the rut of an old routine (yes, I know I am into routines – as long as they continue to be useful) and you have become too comfortable in it. If you took time to review your life plan and vision, you may find that your children have grown up and left the nest, and your plans should have changed but haven't.

When you choose to re-visit and re-organise your personal and family plan is entirely up to you. All I am suggesting is that it is done regularly, both individually and shared collaboratively with significant others. Beware of 'imposing' your life plan on the rest of the tribe. Authentic leadership in meeting all the followers' needs is important. Learning partnerships in co-creating this living document are absolutely crucial here.

Firstly, do you have a personal and family plan drafted? If not, why not draft one right now? If you have a draft of the plan, when did you last dust out the cobwebs of that living document you drafted and left on the shelf? If it is more than five years old, it is definitely worth a revival. Have you scheduled a time-frame for regular re-visits? If you have reviewed the plan, did you share it with someone you respect so he or she can be a part of it and/or support you in realising it? If not, why not? If so, what is the other person's contribution? If you haven't re-visited it, do you plan to do so? When and how?

Businesses tend to do an annual strategic planning

retreat. As a parent, it is just as important to regularly take stock – to review and reflect – whether it is quarterly, monthly, weekly or even daily. Small tweaks make for big changes over time. Have you put this in your routine to reorganise?

One of the key challenges to reorganising or implementing change is: how sustainable is the plan? Why bother to change it if it doesn't stick?

Are you sustaining your changes?

Several Decembers ago, I attended an event where there was a presentation on numerology. We were given numerical formulas based on our birthdates to work out how our energies would vibrate and resonate this year. Out of curiosity and fun, I went ahead and played the game. According to this particular feng shui master's charts, the year ahead for me was one of 'expression'. I was told to exert considerable effort to put my ideas into reality, because creativity, inspiration and imagination were waiting to express themselves the next year. If my creativity was well-directed, the year promised to be financially rewarding. Discipline and focus were the key.

Truly, I am not particularly superstitious. I am one who believes we have a guiding destiny and, paradoxically, have the ability to create any future we choose. So why did I play the numerology game in the first place? Because it was worth an R&R, and possible reorganisation of my life plan. It was another loosening and 'losing of my mind' exercise to shake out any old preconceived ideas, and open up my senses to see what else could be possible.

And maybe it was about needing the energy of pro-pulsion to get me going: if the prophesy were glowing, it might give me a motivating push towards my goals for the year; if it weren't, then it would challenge me to move away from the awful things predicted for the year to prove it all wrong anyway.

Maybe I was unconsciously probing for some tangible sign of the guiding destiny I believe in to point me to what I needed to do. On the other hand, I was hoping to hear something to provoke me into making some deci-sions on what I can achieve the following year.

Could it be that I was looking to collaborate on a higher vision and make it happen in a new way? Perhaps I was just wanting reinforcement of what I choose to hear. Or was it about testing myself to see if I really am as unsuperstitious as I thought?

When it is that time again – as the new year dawns – change is imminent. The two questions I ask of myself are:

1. What changes will manifest this year?
2. How sustainable are the changes?

Whether it is about your business, career, family or personal life, do we not all want to make some worthwhile changes each new year? I suppose that is why New Year's resolutions are so popular all around the world.

Have you ever wondered why most New Year's resolutions do not get acted upon past the week in which they were made? Similarly, what about the rate of success implementing those amazing new ideas you learned from a weekend motivational seminar?

Remedial change versus generative change

There is a model of change for remedial change not based on therapy, but which is structured around transformative and generative change in coaching to peak performance. It is not about the fixing of something broken, but instead it is intended to help direct change in a healthy system, improving it from good to better, and even to extraordinary. The 'axes of change' model was developed by Dr L. Michael Hall and Michelle Duval to create sustainable change in a coaching environment in a systematic and structured way.

As I take you through an overview of the axes of change model, step back and imagine how easily opportunities open up for you as you systematically create sustainable change. But first, consider why you want to make these changes.

- Is it about making some changes in your family that would move everyone from good to great?

- Is it about altering your lifestyle so you get to do more of what you love in your leisure hours and therefore be even more effective at your work?
- Is it about changing some habits that could boost your health in mind, body and spirit?
- Is it about creating more wealth so you can simply have even more freedom of choices in life?
- Is it about making some adjustments to your career or work life so you are doing more of what you love?

The mechanisms of change

According to Hall and Duval, there are eight change factors or variables:

- aversions
- attractions
- reflective understanding
- decision
- creative design
- action
- reinforcement
- testing.

The key mechanisms of generative change work in this manner:

- The negative and positive emotions (aversions and

attractions) to move you away from one thing and compel you towards another.

- The reflective understanding of what needs to change and the decision or commitment to make it happen.
- The creative and constructive phase and designing of what to change internally and then beginning experimentation of the action plan to see how it works in real life.
- The reinforcement of what works by shaping and rewarding it until it is robust enough, followed by a process of ongoing testing, monitoring and accountability that enables the change to continue to improve and to solidify as a new enhancing habit.

At times any one of these factors will be sufficient to create change. You may have experienced it yourself, or seen it work in the life of another – for example, when sufficient pain drove a person to change overnight, such as the patient who has a fear of dentists and who finally turns up because of an excruciating abscess?

Sometimes a great vision awakens a person to new possibilities, creating a sudden transformation. Have you ever been to a seminar where the presenter was so passionate that his or her message made you change something in your life overnight? Perhaps it was about eating healthily or changing careers.

Perhaps the 'aha!' experience creates an immediate

and complete change. Or it could be that receiving some constructive feedback from a colleague, friend or family member gives you the mirror that leads to transformation?

The axes of change

To create sustainable change, you need to become aware of the interrelationships between the eight variables (see list above) and facilitate them accordingly. Think of something you wish to change, and go through these variables – notice how easy it is to make it all happen.

Let's say I wish to get rid of a few of those extra kilograms that crept up on me over Christmas, and keep them off. How will I use the model to self-coach myself back into the clothes in my wardrobe?

The energy (motivation) stage or axis

You need to challenge the current reality – and the aversive consequences if things do not change. Simultaneously, you need to awaken a new vision of possibilities and all the attractive opportunities that change will bring into your life. So I think of all the horrible consequences of staying with the kilos, such as the lack of energy, the compounding of lack of energy and lack of exercise leading to even more weight gain, not looking good or feeling good about myself . . . and I also dare to dream about the activities I can indulge in if I am lean and flexible, not to mention the fabulous new clothes I can buy that will make me feel even more amazing.

191

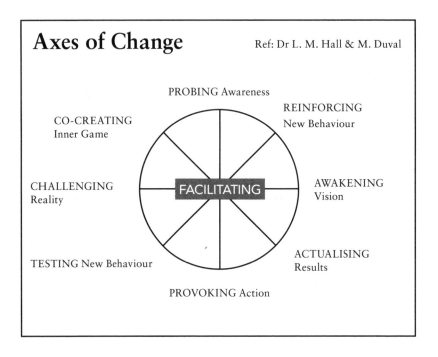

Axes of Change

Ref: Dr L. M. Hall & M. Duval

PROBING Awareness

REINFORCING
New Behaviour

CO-CREATING
Inner Game

CHALLENGING
Reality

FACILITATING

AWAKENING
Vision

TESTING New Behaviour

ACTUALISING
Results

PROVOKING Action

The decision stage or axis

Probe your current understandings and the meaning frames that describe your current behaviours and feelings in order to trigger making a decision to change. At the same time, to create a readiness for making the decision to change, provoke yourself to make a decision to say no to the current state and yes to new possibilities. For me, what really works is to make myself see my current situation as so unbearable I make the decision to act immediately. For example, I face up to the reality that I have *less* options for activities and great clothes and shoes when I am overweight and that is absolutely compelling for me to decide to make that change.

The creation stage or axis

It is useful to have a partner to help design the new strategy and action plan and to imprint the process in your mind and heart. This can involve experimenting and learning and is particularly exciting for me as I love engaging with others to get something happening. I do not just have one buddy to support me through this. I have been known to engage a huge percentage of my email database or my social media network for brainstorming ways to beat stuff like this . . . and celebrating every little win with as many friends as possible.

The solidification stage or axis

Reinforce the new behaviours and responses. Hold yourself accountable, and refine the new changes, gathering new information to feed back into the creation axis. Once again, validate every little step forward (even if you have to say it to yourself in the mirror!) as you shed weight gram by gram and millimetre by millimetre. I always find myself an 'unreasonable' friend who can challenge and call me on my setbacks – and not just coddle me to death. Like, 'Girlfriend, put that chocolate bar back on the shelf!'

Dancing between the axes

Here is an example of how you can reorganise, say, the situation of a stay-at-home mother who is moving back to full-time work. You can attempt to coach her tribe to

get excited about the change, take action to accommo-
date everyone and plan for it to be sustainable:

1. *Energy*: How can you challenge the tribe's current
   reality and awaken attractive new possibilities?
   For example, highlight how frustrated the mother
   is with having two full-time jobs – at home and at
   work – and how that impacts on her interaction
   with the rest of the family. Imagine how the family
   can spend more time together by sharing out home
   duties and, at the same time, relieve the mother's
   stress and home workload. And remind everyone
   how her new income means more finances to pay
   for more fun things or experiences.

2. *Decision*: How can you probe the understanding
   of the current situation for the whole tribe? How
   do you provoke them to say no to the current situation and yes to reorganising?

3. *Creation*: This is when the tribe is ready to brainstorm some ways to reorganise and have buy-in
   about trying the new action plan and commit-
   ting to giving it a go. Permission for it not to go
   perfectly is fine – that is still permission to make
   changes and trial new ways.

4. *Solidification*: This is when you support the process to test and reinforce what is going right, and
   give feedback and make new changes as you go.
   The agreement charter with the whole family
   becomes important. The whole process is organic

and happens through constant conversation.

The first three steps can probably occur in a two-hour session with the tribe. The last step is likely to occur over a more extended 'trial' period as the new reorganised mode is put into play.

As you dance through the axes of change model, can you now see how a lot of those New Year's resolutions could have been achieved? It is a matter of putting the resolution through a structure that naturally facilitates the changes to occur.

So, what are you waiting for? Go and reorganise those goals. Work through the axes of change for each of them, and notice how many more you can fulfil by the time the next year comes in.

Parent as coach

You can also use this model to coach your children, or your co-parent, or any playpals, to help them achieve what they want. Enjoy dancing.

Just *do* it. It is all about choice.

Applying the three Rs of partnering skills

With reorganising, it is important to constantly keep your wits and senses about you to tweak as you go:

1. *Reading*: Dance between doing and stepping back to get a sense of how the reorganising is going.
2. *Righting*: If all is going well, stay on the new plan.
3. *Re-writing*: Tweak and re-write the plan as the reorganising is happening.

So what are you doing to transform the R&R agreements into a reorganised action plan in your family?

Dos and don'ts

Do experiment

Children learn their own language by experimenting with sound, with writing and with spelling. Their experimentation with musical sounds is no different. Encourage them to find tunes and rhythms for themselves in different areas of life – for example, let them crinkle a baguette and listen for the tone the bread crust makes. Let them enjoy listening to the patter of rain – and make up a rhyme or story to the beat. Children learn from imaginative behaviour. Exploratory behaviour is part of a successful environment. Encourage them to be curiouser and curiouser . . . and through the looking glass they go!

Do encourage any behaviour that is a move in the right direction

Remember how long it took for your child to learn to talk. Remember how you encouraged any sound that was remotely like a word. If a child shows an interest in a musical instrument, encourage them to sit at the piano or take the violin out of its case and feel the bow. Let them listen to recordings of masterpieces and encourage them to identify the instruments in the recordings. Make it fun.

'Starting children off with the fun of playing a game, letting their spirit of fun lead them in the right direction, is the way all education of children should be started,' said Dr Shinichi Suzuki. No exceptions in any contexts.

Adults often want to know the 'why' of learning; children mostly want to learn. They learn through seeing, doing, hearing, feeling, tasting and smelling. They do things because they are there to do. They do things that feel good. They do things they enjoy. They do things that are fun.

Don't forget posture and balance

Through a balanced body a child will develop the ability to do a variety of things without tension, and from this will flow coordination. Whether it is sports, playing a musical instrument, doing mental arithmetic or reading, posture – along with listening, watching (modelling) and practice – is important to cultivate ability. When you learn a language well, you learn the gestures that native speakers use – for example, the French 'shrug' or the Italian 'embrace' – and these help you speak with the correct intonation or rhythm; when you play tennis, you need to know how to lean into the ball and how to swing the racquet.

'The head and the body have to work together,' said Dr Suzuki. 'I believe that a human being is formed through the great activity of life, through absorbing from the environment.'

Personal learning journal

What is at least one thing you learned about yourself from this lesson?

1.

Write down at least one thing you will implement immediately.

1.

TEN

Running It: Response-ability

Now that you have a system of continuous improvement, through 'thinking' and 'doing', it is useful to run these processes in conjunction with the ability to respond with ease and grace. This is about your ability to respond, and about managing the processes:

1. role-modelling
2. respect
3. rules
4. routine
5. review and reflect (R&R)
6. reorganise.

Running the seven Rs of parenting with response-ability means leading a great life yourself to excite your family members to unleash their highest potential through exceptional actions. It is about your ability to respond to the 'business-as-usual' day-to-day goings on, as well as the unusual and the unforeseen that get thrown your way. After all, you live in a world of exponential change.

It is also about helping your children become more response-able. Hopefully, through role-modelling, they will be picking up a lot of this instinctively – as per Massey's model (see page 36). If you are aware, you can certainly guide them – remembering that this is a learning partnership. If both parents and children are open and highly sensible – that is, 'sense-able', or able to come to their senses to read a situation – as well as able to respond to changing contexts, it will be a very efficient organic system of sustainable operations and change.

But, it ain't gonna happen on its own. So this is about the 'doing' part of parenting. This is the engine-room stuff. The daily operations of working the life plan. It is a cycle of accountability, monitoring, tweaking, actioning.

It starts with you, the parent, being responsible (or 'response-able') for knowing and *respecting* yourself enough. Have you considered and clearly defined your life vision? What makes this meaningful and purposeful enough to excite you and your family to come with you? What are the values you will not compromise? How does this realisation impact your behaviour? What is the first step to *lead a great life* – the first for you, and then with respect to the family? For those who take planes often, remember the constant reminder about putting on the oxygen mask first before helping others.

Next, how do you *role-model to leave a legacy* of loving and living a great life? It is not about making your children multiple clones of you and your life. It is your authenticity that inspires them to, in turn, lead a great life according to how they define it.

Making sure you are aware of the *rules* that drive your behaviours unconsciously is important. Rewrite those rules that no longer serve you. Make these new and useful rules come alive for you and those you love and care for. Having clear boundaries is a cornerstone for self-esteem, independence, trust and connectedness. Partnering to create and commit to a family charter according to your rules, beliefs and values means you can enforce, and reinforce, the behaviours you have agreed to live by in times of conflict, in times of difficulties about decisions, derisions and delinquency.

You can then collaborate to create *routines* to enable things to run efficiently and effectively – with ease and grace. Routines free you up to be more spontaneous and creative.

Reviewing and reflecting (R&R) give you the opportunity to learn from one another – and to continuously improve. They help you to live daily moments of bliss and connectedness by celebrating wins and learnings often: *to leave things or people better than when you found them.* R&R can help your family's purpose or mission statement in a variety of ways.

Paul Mitchell, a good friend and well-respected colleague in leadership facilitation, always impressed this on his charges: *Come in early as a partner, not late as a judge.* It is only through the regular 'practice of the pause' that you can stop, review and reflect (R&R) and seek this learning partnership thoughtfully and openly.

Reorganise. Review and reflect constantly, leading to reorganising, is the natural course of things. Make small tweaks and celebrate often. An ancient Chinese proverb states, 'The thousand *li* journey begins with the first step.' Take courage to take the first step. The next step comes easier, no matter how enormous any change may prove to be in the long run. Just focus on the first step – it is always a change for the better. Reorganising begins with the first step.

So what are you doing about *running it* – your life plan? Without losing your authenticity, how *response-able* are you to changing circumstances?

Since this is about the management of self and your family/team, it comes back to the 'think–do–get' model, which allows you to be consistent in your responses.

THINK ⟹ DO ⟹ GET

Why do we mostly let life run us with regard to families instead of putting some structure in place so everybody knows where we are going and what we care about? If you do not put a structure in place that allows you to work towards how you would like things to be ideally, you end up letting life run you. Sure, there is much to be said for spontaneity and seeing what surprises there are in store. However, how would you know the great unexpected if you did not have expectations of how it should be in the first place?

Being a playpal means managing yourself before everybody else does.

Your response-ability is related to how well you are running yourself or your family.

Reading the self: responsibility to and for . . .

You have a responsibility to provide the best environment for your family, but each person has a responsibility for their individual actions. It is important to instil this accountability for self in your children as early as possible.

Goffee and Jones summed this up well: 'Be yourself – more – with skill.' Know yourself enough. Show yourself enough, depending on the context. As much as you are comfortable with your origins, strengths, values and life experiences, it is just as important to be vulnerable (in the appropriate context) so that your family can step up to help you when you need help. Hence, they see you as authentically human, and feel significant to be part of your trusted community to help you. I am not suggesting for a moment you need your daily lives to be like an episode on a confessional television show. Show yourself – enough: that's the key. It's an easy concept, but difficult to execute. It takes practice, practice, practice.

Let's be mindful of some of the following:

1. Why do you want to lead? Describe your intentions.
2. Describe the environment/culture you would like to cultivate as your family's leader. Is it strictly authoritarian top-down management? Or is it collaborative empowerment? Perhaps a mixture, depending on the ages of your children and the experience of family members?
3. What behaviours would you ideally exhibit as a leader? Do you have a 'civil code' of behaviour and expectations with a consistent set of consequences? If so, please write these down where it is easily visible to the family. Make time to explain it clearly to the family, if you have not done so already.
4. What capabilities do you possess as a leader? What do you need to develop? What are the weaknesses you feel you can show your family so they can step up and help you?
5. Do you have ways to celebrate achievement, to inspire ambition, to count every little win in your family? If so, list at least three ways.
6. Are you aware of your beliefs and values? If so, list your top five beliefs and values.
7. Have you shared your vision, values and purpose in life with your family? If not, why not? If so, how have the vision, values and purpose been created

(for example, are they all from you or were they co-created in a family collaboration)? When were they last re-visited?

8. What is your identity in the parenting role: dictator, mentor, teacher, counsellor, consultant, therapist, rescuer, facilitator, coach, director, martyr, follower, drama king/queen, warrior, equal? List five benefits and five drawbacks of that identity.

9. What is the context/spirituality/philosophy by which you lead a great life? Can you 'walk your talk', 'live your values', 'role-model' it to your family? If so, give three examples of how you do this.

As parents, you are joint managing directors of the household (whether your children are biological or step-children). You lead the household with pride. You work together to run a fair management system, with rules and routine that they understand. Everybody is then happy.

There are variations to this. There are co-parents who have chosen to parent apart – it is like leading virtual teams and takes a lot more effort, organisation and clear communication. It can be done well, or not. It's a choice.

It is more difficult for single parents. One person has to play both roles of masculine and feminine leadership . . . but it too can be done successfully. Being authentic is crucial, as is showing your allowable weaknesses so your children can step up to support you. Otherwise they will invent your flaws, or follow the so-called MIUAYGA principle (that is, 'make it up as you go along').

The other side of the coin is that what you have at home you can bring to work as well: leadership from the heart – how can you love your team more? What if you had a team that you could but did not want to sack? How would you behave differently with them? What if you gave them the resources – limited or not – that allowed them to become the best they could be, even if you knew that they would leave sooner or later? You may even hope that they find a bigger or better pond to play in because you want to 'leave them better than you found them'. How would that impact world industry?

You may be beginning to see how an authentic leader brings all of him or herself into the many contexts of existence, and chooses to show enough of self by reading situations correctly and then 'righting' or re-writing them according to what is most appropriate.

How does it work?

You may notice how all six principles come alive and into their own as I describe the variety of approaches we have been using to 'run it' in our family. Try picking out where role-modelling, respect, rules, routine, R&R and reorganise principles come into play:

1. *Independence*: I valued my independence as my parents 'slowly released the apron strings', giving me and my siblings more and more response-ability as

we grew up. In order to nurture that independence in Jett and Xian, I give them this same opportunity. For example, they can keep their own rooms in any state they want. I agree not to go in to clean or tidy. So if they lose stuff in their mess, they need to find it. They also make their own lunches. So if they forget, they go hungry, or pay for lunch from their own pocket money.

2. *The law*: which has been in place since my children were born.

   a. All family members are to treat each other with respect – for example, no screaming, hitting, verbal or physical abuse. Penalty: time out according to age (that is, one year equals one minute time out) *or* privileges revoked (see Chapter 6: Rules).

   b. Safety rules are prescribed by parents for the children's protection – for example, no electrical sockets to be touched, cross roads with adult, mount stairs with hand on rails, in bed at curfew. Penalty: time out *or* privileges revoked.

3. *The civil code*: A set of guidelines that are displayed in a common living area (see Chapter 6, page 92):

   a. For appropriate conduct, 'points' are awarded.

   b. Inappropriate conduct invokes a 'removal of points' by the same number – for example, hitting a person to snatch a toy may invoke 'removal of four points'; sharing a toy voluntarily will be awarded four points.

c. Privileges decided by child can be 'exchanged' for a preset system of 'points'.

4. *Responsibilities*: Responsibilities are rewarded regularly with privileges earned from doing particular tasks well. For example, letting children have thirty minutes unsupervised adult-free time has become a privilege (naturally, they are able to call us by mobile phone if any crisis does arise); before this privilege was tried, there has been discussions involving health and safety guidelines (for example, in case of fire, what to do, where to meet, who to call, etc). So now the children have adult-free time of up to two hours in our apartment.

So what are you doing about *running it* – your life plan? Without losing your authenticity, how *response-able* are you to changing circumstances?

Applying the three Rs of partnering skills

In executing the seven Rs of parenting, notice how important it is to hone your sensory awareness skills in order to be constantly dancing in and out to manage running it with response-ability:

1. *Reading*: Dance between the dance floor 'doing' and 'stepping back' on the balcony – in order to

get a sense of how you are running it and respond-
ing to changes.

2. *Righting*: If all is going well, stay on the plan.
3. *Re-writing*: Tweak and re-write the plan as you cycle
from R&R to Reorganising.

So what are you doing to manage putting all the seven Rs
together in your family?

Dos and don'ts

Do co-create learning partnerships with children

It is natural for parents to be the 'teacher' but look for
opportunities to learn from your kids.

For example, children are naturally curious and see the
world in wonder and awe, so learn from them as they are
appreciating the beauty of the world through the simplest
things: sifting sand, running in bare feet, not caring whether
or not they sing out of tune or dance off rhythm. Adults can
rediscover this aspect of themselves. And notice how rep-
etition is natural for children – adults give up too quickly.

Do excite your children to exceptional performance

In their book *Why Should Anyone Be Led by You?*, Rob
Goffee and Gareth Jones describe the effective leader
as one who understands what the followers need – and
excites them to exceptional performances without losing their authenticity. It sounds simple. Yet it does take

effort. Parenting is leadership. And it is a labour of love. As we know with children (and adults alike), when you feel understood, you are more likely to be led.

Do be a purposeful parent

Don't stop learning

Do be passionate

Do love life

Personal learning journal

Write down thoughts/feelings you had from this lesson.

1.

2.

3.

4.

Write down at least one thing you will implement immediately.

1.

PART THREE

Leading and Learning

ELEVEN

Applying the Seven Rs of Parenting to *Your* Life

During a recent holiday season, I was at a Christmas cocktail party mingling with some colleagues who are principals in a professional services firm. The typical lament I heard from them was that it is impossible to motivate some team members but easy to motivate others. One colleague commented that he could not motivate one staff member, yet another of his managers seemed to be able to do so, and vice versa. He asked, 'Could it be that our leadership styles are different?' It seemed so. The question I asked him was, 'Do you know what your leadership style is and how do you make it work for you, or not?'

What is true in business is equally true at home. To be a great leader of your tribe you need to understand exactly which leadership style you have. And applying the seven Rs of parenting requires leadership from *you*.

Inspiring a call to action

Visionary leaders can have great strategies. However, if they cannot express these strategies to inspire and engage their followers (let alone execute those ideas), unfortunately their vision fails. How can a leader inspire a call to action? It begins with being able to transmit the message so that the followers will clearly receive it on their wavelength. If a leader prefers a different channel, and is not able to adapt his or her style to connect to the rest of the tribe, the communication inevitably fails.

Let me run this question by you too. Do you consciously know *how* you lead and inspire your tribe at home to action, or is it just hit and miss? Would you be interested if there was a way of identifying your strengths and weaknesses in motivating yourself and your team? Would you be curious about how you can turn your weaknesses into strengths? Would you like to be so flexible that you can learn to manage all members of your tribe by adopting the style that best fits the tribe at any moment in time?

Sounds too good to be true? It isn't really. You do need to put in some hard yards to discover which style you default to, and you must be ready to try other styles when the situation demands it. Ready?

Learning styles

The American educator Bernice McCarthy developed the 4MAT system to help teachers maximise learning by integrating the different learning styles of students in classrooms. She found that teachers were very much acting as motivators, coaches and mentors using this system. It works just as well for a parent motivating the tribe at home.

Let us look at this in a little bit more detail and see whether you can identify your learning and leadership preferences from the descriptions. You may notice some of these styles in the people you work with and those you live with at home. The styles that you are least comfortable with are those you most need to develop to become more inspiring.

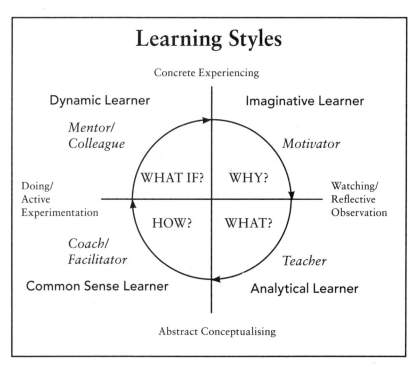

The imaginative learner/leader

These leaders tend to perceive information concretely and process reflectively. They integrate experience with the self. They learn by listening and sharing ideas. They discuss ideas to achieve a level of collaboration. They are imaginative thinkers who believe in their own experience. They excel in viewing direct experience from many perspectives. They value insightful thinking. They work for harmony, a sense of belonging, inclusion and fairness.

They need to be personally involved, seek commitment and are interested in people and culture. They are thoughtful people who enjoy observing others. They absorb reality; they seem to take in the atmosphere almost by osmosis.

But, being 'people' people, their need to be liked may threaten progress. Their desire for consensus can be limiting.

As leaders, they:

- thrive on taking time to develop good ideas
- tackle problems by reflecting alone and then brainstorming with staff
- lead from their heart and involve other people in decision-making
- exercise authority with trust and participation
- work for organisational solidarity
- need staff who are supportive and share their sense of mission.

Their strength: innovation and ideas
They function by: value clarification
Their goals: to be involved in important issues and to bring harmony
Their best role: motivator
Their favourite question: why?

The analytical learner/leader

These leaders perceive information abstractly and process it reflectively. They form theories and concepts by integrating their observations into what is known. They seek continuity. They need to know what the experts think. They learn by thinking through ideas. They value sequential thinking. They need details. They critique information and collect data. They are thorough and industrious. They will re-examine the facts if a situation perplexes them. They enjoy traditional classrooms. Schools are made for them.

However, paralysis by analysis could be a limitation. They are more interested in ideas than people. They prefer to maximise certainty and are uncomfortable with subjective judgements. Being credible is important.

As leaders, they:

- thrive on assimilating disparate facts into coherent theories
- tackle problems with rationality and logic
- lead by principles and procedures

- exercise authority with assertive persuasion, by knowing the facts
- work to enhance their organisation as an embodiment of tradition and prestige
- need staff who are well organised, have things down on paper and follow through on agreed decisions.

Their strength: creating concepts and models
They function by: thinking things through
Their goals: intellectual recognition
Their best role: teacher
Their favourite question: what?

The common sense learner/leader

These leaders perceive information abstractly and process it actively. They integrate theory and practice. They learn by testing theories and applying common sense. They are pragmatists who believe that if something works use it. They are down-to-earth problem-solvers who resent being given answers. They do not stand on ceremony but get right to the point. They have a limited tolerance for fuzzy ideas. They value strategic thinking. They are skills oriented. They experiment and tinker with things. They need to know how things work. They edit reality, cut right to the heart of things. They want to get down and just do. This can be a disadvantage – they may sometimes plant seeds before the ground is fertilised, in a shoot-first, aim-second kind of way. They can sometimes seem bossy and impersonal.

As leaders, they:

- thrive on plans and timelines
- tackle problems by making unilateral decisions
- lead by personal forcefulness, inspiring quality
- exercise authority by reward/punishment (the fewer the rules the better, but they enforce them)
- work hard to make their organisation productive and solvent
- need staff who are task-oriented and move quickly.

Their strength: practical application of ideas

They function by: factual data garnered from kinesthetic, hands-on experience

Their goals: to align their view of the present with future security

Their best role: coach, facilitator

Their favourite question: how?

The dynamic learner/leader

These leaders perceive information concretely and process it actively. They integrate experience and application. They learn by trial and error. They are believers in self-discovery. They are enthusiastic about new things. They are creative, adaptable and even relish change. They are constantly reinventing the wheel, almost doing it for 'difference' sake, to develop to yet another level. They are constantly stimulated, do not like letting things lie and may lack focus. They excel when flexibility is needed.

They can be accused of being 'loose cannons', free-wheeling with little planning and preparation: 'I think I'll wing it' is a typical comment. They often reach accurate conclusions in the absence of logical justification. They are risk-takers. They are at ease with people. They enrich reality by taking what is and adding to it. Sometimes they are seen as manipulative and pushy.

As leaders, they:

- thrive on crisis and challenge
- tackle problems by looking for patterns, scanning possibilities
- lead by energising people
- exercise authority by holding up visions of what might be
- work hard to enhance their organisation's reputation
- need staff who can follow up and implement details.

Their strengths: action, getting things going
They function by: acting and testing experience
Their goals: to bring action to ideas
Their best role: mentor, colleague
Their favourite question: what if?

Putting it all together

Let's see how we can put those styles in a meaningful contrast to illustrate their differences. Take, for example, a typical family Christmas Eve scenario. The leader (you) has been down to the shop and bought a bike for Santa to deliver on Christmas morning. The only problem is that it is in a box and needs to be put together. How you respond to this challenge indicates exactly what kind of leader you are.

If you are an *imaginative leader*, you will ring up your friends to come and help put it together. You will be likely to lobby and motivate them to come over (by consensus of course) by giving them 101 reasons *why* it will be beneficial for all to do this project together. When the collaborative process of putting it together is complete using everybody's expertise fairly, you celebrate by breaking out the mince pies as you place the wrapped bike under the tree together. A sense of community is vital to you. In order that there is inclusion, and that you remain liked, you also let everyone involved know that they can come back tomorrow and enjoy the look of joy on junior's face when the bicycle is unwrapped.

If you are an *analytical leader*, you will first sit down and unwrap the box. You will read through the accompanying manual carefully from cover to cover to determine *what* needs to be done. If you have any enthusiastic friends or family around wanting to dive into the assembly, you tell them that they have to remain patient while

221

you organise, identify and sort out the parts and the procedure according to the printed instructions. Once you have your facts, you then organise who you perceive to be best at specific procedures, and arrange them in an assembly line to put the bike together. You are in your element if you can *teach* them how to do this by taking them through the manual, step by step. Once the bicycle is put together, you complete a checklist of details before the best rider in the group road tests it (you will naturally obtain evidence from your team to find out who is the best) before carefully placing the bike, at a predetermined optimum point, under the tree.

The *common sense leader* will want to get down and just do it! The box is ripped apart and the manual tossed aside – only to be referred to if you get really stuck. You quickly assemble people around you into task groups: one to handle the mobile elements such as handlebars and wheels, another for the mechanical parts such as pedals, brakes, chain and gears. Your brief to the teams is simple: just put it together as efficiently and quickly as possible. You remind them that they all know what a bike looks like – *how* to put it together is just common sense. You will jump in to coach/facilitate them when they run into problems – referring to the instructions manual is the last resort. You hate being asked 'stupid questions'. When the bicycle is fully assembled, it is whipped under the tree while you start looking for the next project to work on. It is not that you do not acknowledge the great performance of the team: it is your assumption that the well-assembled bike is evidence enough to the team that they have done well.

Should you, the *dynamic leader*, get into the project, you will find that you are likely to challenge your team to take a journey of self-discovery. You will throw away the packaging and the manual with it. You will challenge your people first to nominate what it is you are assembling based on the parts laid out. Once all of you have made a collegiate decision that it is a bicycle, you expect them to discover what is the best way of putting it together, without the instructions. Your aim is to mentor them to build a bike that is unique. *What if* we put the handlebars where the saddle usually is? What if the wheels were not in the same plane? What if they were parallel rather than the usual tandem set-up? What if it cannot be ridden at all? What if there is another use for this 'different' vehicle other than being a bicycle? That will make for an interesting reaction on Christmas morning.

Are you now seeing yourself in one of the styles? So what does it all mean? How does being aware of your intuitive leadership style impact on you inspiring your tribe to action? Or not?

Learning styles of your team

Just as your leadership style is linked to your learning preference, your team's preferred learning style also impacts their response-ability to how you lead, manage and inspire them. The same characteristics and traits that define how you lead also identify how you learn.

At home, a dynamic learner in the family tribe may perceive an analytical leader to be anally retentive, overwhelmingly boring and frustrating. This dynamic, experiential, inventive tribal member thrives on making a difference by being creative and actually thinks that the time spent on changing the systems over and over is smart. By contrast, the detailed, analytical, procedural leader considers the dynamic member to be a drama queen, who wastes time on mundane things and is a loose cannon who does not follow the rules.

Or say you have a son who is an imaginative learner, whose mother is a common sense leader. This practical, just-get-it-done, hands-on mum may be perceived as bossy and impersonal by the son, who prefers a more inclusive, communal sense of collaboration leadership and who expects a more overt acknowledgement of a job well done. He just needs a kind word and a pat on the back, Ma!

Starting to see a pattern here?

Managing a diverse team

You can now see that as a leader, you do not just manage people who have similar learning styles. When it happens – great! In that case, the team finds it easy to understand and work together. An ideal team is a combination of people who complement one another with their differing strengths. For example, in the Learning Styles above, a team with the same homogenous style will likely have many blind spots. A diverse team is probably going to experience more conflict due to the differences, but the different strengths of each style augments and complements one another. Child psychologists believe that each child in a family tends to develop different ways of gaining attention from the parents – so is it any wonder that there are so many differences in behaviour, personality and learning styles in the children of each family unit?

How do you manage this diversity?

The leader, having become aware of his or her default leadership style, then learns to adapt that style to suit each member – in order to motivate every individual to come on board, implement changes, realise a new vision or just simply to get along.

How to incorporate the learning styles into your leadership

1. Become aware of your preferred learning/leadership style – be it imaginative, analytical, common sense or dynamic.
2. Develop your three non-preferred learning styles – using the roles of motivator, teacher, coach/facilitator, and mentor/colleague as a guide.
3. Incorporate and flex across all four learning styles

into your leadership – using the relevant questions of why? what? how? and what if? appropriately when rallying your tribe.

To illustrate how this works let's use what happened with the businessman at the Christmas cocktail party who was concerned about his leadership style.

After I described to him the different 4MAT learning/leadership styles, he decided that he was more of a common sense leader. Upon further reflection, he realised how the different people who bugged him tended to prefer the other three learning styles. He also recognised that his office manager was more an imaginative leader. Hence, he could see how some team members would be more amenable to her style, and vice versa.

I described how each style corresponded best to particular roles (motivator, teacher, coach/facilitator or mentor/colleague) and their favourite questions of why? what? how? and what if? He found it useful to start developing his motivator, teacher and mentor/colleague sides in order to reach the other team members who did not respond to his coach/facilitator style. Keeping the four favourite questions in mind was another easy way to jog his memory of what to say. If he wasn't sure which learning style each team member inclined towards, he could use the questions in a sentence to jog his memory.

It's a matter of flexibility

The more flexible the leader, the easier it is to align tribal members with the purpose of the family and facilitate productivity and efficiency by bringing out the best in everybody.

So, the next time you encounter barriers to changes you wish to put in place in your family – such as resistance to a new vision or family members who seem abrasive and difficult to motivate – why not reflect upon yourself to see whether you are defaulting to your preferred leadership style? Imagine what it would be like to appreciate and take on the four different learning styles. Incorporate them into your call to action to inspire your family's heart and soul to come along with you.

Understanding these learning styles can help in the learning partnerships as a playpal. Using the three Rs of partnering, you can now:

1. *Read* the learning style: observe what is the wavelength by which the information you want to convey to the tribe will be best channelled and, hence, clearly received.
2. *Right* the learning style: you can match the channel by delivering the message in the style(s) appropriate to the tribe. If unsure, covering all bases is a useful strategy.
3. *Re-write* the context: you may find that the metaphor or structure you are using to deliver the

message is not inspiring this particular tribe. Using the 'right' styles, you can alter the form, analogy or story to inspire without changing the meaning of the message you want to convey.

Trust now that you can begin to motivate, inspire and lead your tribe in any direction you choose to take your business or your family. So the next time you come up against what in the past would have seemed a barrier to any changes in your life, consider it an exciting new opportunity to further develop your motivational intelligence.

Equality of the sexes?

One subject that constantly comes up when discussing parenting or leadership is the question of gender. Is there a difference between female and male leadership styles? Is one style better than the other?

In an ideal family dynamic, the father is usually the yang leader, and the mother is the yin leader. If the context calls for yin leadership – when collaboration is necessary – then the feminine side steps up. If competitive high-risk action is called for, then it is the yang leadership that comes to the fore. Let's take it to leadership in general. Case in point: President Barack Obama is physiologically male and his Secretary of State Hillary Clinton is female. However, I see President Obama's style of leadership as more feminine (yin) and Secretary Clinton's as more masculine (yang).

Neither yin nor yang leadership is better. It just is. The synergy of the two is what is called for in ideal family or tribal dynamics. It is a template of how leadership shifting is normal – and excellent for role-modelling.

However, leadership styles can cause conflict if one is more dominant than the other. The key is balance. Naturally, for a single parent, this creates a challenge of imbalance. How do you manage this?

Single parents who co-parent apart can still create a balance. It just needs more effort in coordination, communication and logistics. Single parents can re-partner – and this again is like a business merger that needs strategic planning and execution so that the family remains engaged as a unit. Those who choose to parent alone need to play both yin and yang roles. This naturally comes with its challenges.

Distinguishing feminine and masculine leadership qualities

I was conferring with business colleagues about how we as leaders of today can transform the next generation. Were there any differences between the sexes in leadership qualities, strengths, weaknesses, opportunities, threats? Oh dear, you must be thinking – she's not opening that old Pandora's box on the battle of the sexes again?

Breathe easy. I really do not want to go there. What I

want to do is provoke some thoughts and feelings around these differences so that you can harness any obvious strengths and talents over your vulnerabilities. Women/men, Venus/Mars, yin/yang . . . they exist in nature to complement one another. Neither is good or bad, they just are. Are women or men better leaders? Their combined yin and yang leadership styles are essentially a balance of energies. Together, the sum of the parts is greater than the whole. It's synergy at its best. We need both.

What this means for our tribe

Regardless of what gender you are or which style is your preference, let me show you how you can use your strengths to your advantage (and therefore that of the family you lead). Yin leadership does not have to be only for women. You can learn from both the yin and the yang, so that a balanced leadership style embraces the qualities of both. Awareness creates choice, permitting appropriate qualities to be applied in different contexts.

In history, yang leadership has been rewarded. So much so that women in power had to accentuate their more masculine competitive streak. Think of Margaret Thatcher, Queen Elizabeth I, Empress Dowager Cixi, Joan of Arc.

I believe understanding yin and yang leadership allows the two to work as complementary styles through which you not only can develop yourself, but transform leaders of tomorrow.

Family leadership is about co-parenting with both styles. When single parents are forced to be both things for their children, it can be exceptionally challenging. Let us not regard one style being better than the other – because different contexts bring out the strengths of each one. Look at synergising the two so that you get the best of both as playpals.

TWELVE

Are Parents Heroes?

Heroes. What do they mean to you? Do images of mythical heroes like Sir Lancelot of the Round Table, the Chinese warrior Hua Mulan, the Greek immortal Psyche or Luke Skywalker the Jedi knight spring to mind? Could it be legends of history like Joan of Arc, Alexander the Great, Genghis Khan, Marie Curie? Or is it about the superheroes like Batman, Spiderman, Superman, The Incredibles and, more recently, Ironman? Who are your heroes?

I had this discussion about our greatest heroes with my playpals. We were considering Mahatma Gandhi against Jesus Christ, our own less known yet undoubtedly pioneering great-grandparents and Jacqueline Kennedy Onassis to Steve Jobs. One of my insightful friends piped up, 'Me. I am my greatest hero.' There was a pregnant pause as we all reflected. We tend to look beyond ourselves for heroes – people we admire and aspire to emulate. It was thought-provoking to think that we can be our own greatest hero. And why ever not? Particularly in the context of being a role model – as leaders of our family.

The American Joseph Campbell, who analysed the world's myths and religions and re-introduced us to the mythical sense of the world, said, 'Life is not a problem to be solved but a mystery to be lived . . . It's not the agony of the quest, but the rapture of the revelation.'

Campbell, in contrast to conventional scholars' emphasis on cultural differences, concentrated on similarities in his comparative historical approach to mythology, religion and literature. In his book *The Hero with a Thousand Faces,* he described the poet's way of reading a myth: symbolically, metaphorically, soulfully. In his cross-cultural explorations of the essence of human nature, Campbell consistently alluded to the 'hero's journey' as being a common theme in myths across all cultures. In fact, Hollywood screenwriters have used the formula of the hero's journey to structure movies time and time again.

Since fiction imitates life, is the idea that we are all on a hero's journey far-fetched? If not, am I not the mystery I am seeking to know? Or is that too deep?

Let's break down the hero's journey and see how it applies to your life. In my interpretation of Campbell's thoughts, I consider my life to be one big hero's journey that consists of fragments of countless heroic journeys within. Just one example in my life helps to illuminate the concepts within the hero's journey. As one cycle of this mini-journey ends, a whole new adventure begins at a different level.

Before we embark on our travels together, how do you see yours as a hero's journey?

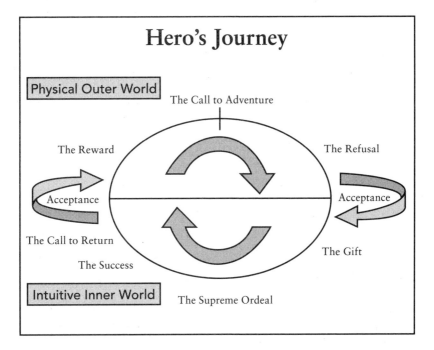

Hero's Journey

Physical Outer World

The Call to Adventure

The Reward

The Refusal

Acceptance

Acceptance

The Call to Return

The Gift

The Success

Intuitive Inner World

The Supreme Ordeal

The call to adventure

It all starts with 'the call'. I am sure we are all familiar with people getting their 'calling'. That's just one way of looking at it.

I began my professional life in dentistry. It was certainly rewarding financially, intellectually and socially. As years went by, I developed not just into working with pediatric dentistry patients but a particular ability to deal with phobic and highly anxious children. I was especially good with hyperventilating kids and their parents. My practice thrived as word got around about how I could transform the lives of these apprehensive patients and their families.

Was this then my calling? Ah. But it is not as obvious. The call to adventure, I believe, really occurred after I got married, and the next step was the question hounding me: 'You're great with kids – so when are you going to be a mother?' The call to the adventure of parenting . . .

The refusal

This is the usual reaction of the hero: 'refusal' to take the call because 'I can't do it' or 'I'm too comfortable to change the status quo' or 'I just do not have the skills.'

In *Star Wars* Luke Skywalker, who was a farmer on his planet, refused to heed Princess Leia's holographic call for help because it was harvest time. Being a warrior was far from his mind. How could it be a calling?

My refusal to the call? In the true form of the career woman of my generation, I was having too good a time to be silly enough to opt out of what all my feminist foremothers had fought so hard to get. So I indulged in 'me, myself and I'. I refused to give up the good life of a career and the self-satisfaction of being a totally independent woman of substance. Kids – forget it. Aren't they supposed to be dependent on you? What would become of my freedom? Besides, I was just a kid myself. How could I look after another soul?

So seven years passed me by, child-free. My mother-in-law gave up pestering me on the baby issue after she asked me to go visit a doctor to see 'if you are having problems with conceiving'. Naughty me, I whispered, 'I have seen a doctor. He said I am fine. I am having trouble getting your son to see him. Would you help me ask him to do so?' With that, she never asked me about having babies again.

Acceptance: transition to intuitive inner world from the physical outer world

Despite all my excuses and justifications, deep down I wanted to be a mother. It just did not feel right at that point in time. The time was, of course, never right. So what the heck – I decided to throw caution to the wind. I accepted the call.

Lo and behold! I was blessed with the conception of my son Jett. But even when my GP confirmed the pregnancy (after the shock of the home test result), I was still in denial. 'My life as I know it is ended!' I remember lamenting to the wide-eyed doctor, who was contemplating registering me as her first antenatal depressive patient.

As you accept the call, you are given a gift. In *Star Wars*, most people think it was the light saber given to Skywalker by Obi-Wan Kenobi. It was actually something more intangible. This gift manifests itself only in the supreme ordeal (see below) – when one's true talent is ultimately tested. Until then, it is hidden within itself.

The gift

As I let go of my personal crisis about not being good enough, or even ready, to be a mother, I decided to embrace parenting with the strong intention of personal development for myself and my child. I thought that was a good frame of mind to come from. Amazingly, I was given a 'gift' then and it remained hidden from me until I was challenged with further ordeals. That is the nature of the gift that is presented to you when you accept the call.

The supreme ordeal

In *Star Wars*, Luke Skywalker encounters many ordeals, which he overcomes, usually with help from a multitude of guides (Obi-Wan Kenobi, Yoda, Han Solo). Facing his 'supreme ordeal' of destroying the Death Star space station (or be annihilated himself), he trusts in the gift of – you guessed it – the Force.

The supreme ordeal brings us to the edge of our beliefs, values and even our identity. We are given the opportunity of a challenge to essentially do ('Use the Force, Luke') or die (if we did not trust to use the hidden gift).

In my case, my prenatal belief was that 'parenting is damn hard and tough work'. I was very unsure whether the selflessness of motherhood was a value I possessed. I was trying on the identity of a mother-to-be and was highly anxious about my ability to do it well. So with those frames of mind, it was no wonder I developed hypertension in my third trimester! Talk about ordeals.

Among the many guides that appeared in this gestation period, one stood out for me. My friend Lis Ainsworth gave me a book by Glen Doman, a child brain developmentalist, called *How to Multiply Your Baby's Intelligence*. Doman talked to me in a way that brought about a paradigm shift in my prenatal belief. I changed it to 'parenting is joyful, natural and I am the best person for my child in his/her learning'.

My supreme ordeal occurred during the delivery of my son. My blood pressure was climbing, despite the epidural working. My obstetrician Ric knew that this could both be a danger to me (should a stroke develop) as well as to the unborn child (who was signalling foetal distress on the monitors). Despite our earlier agreement not to go with a caesarian, I heard Ric order the operating theatre be prepared.

'No!' I could hear myself scream inside my head. 'I

can do this. We can do this, Jett. This is going to be easy. Help me, Jett.' I calmly made this known to the staff and Ric. With the last contraction, Jett started descending through the birth canal and I seemed to hear him communicate to me, 'Don't worry. I have my own destiny – and nothing you do will change that. Just hold the space for me and I will achieve my purpose. You can't do wrong. Just be yourself and I will be fine.'

It may sound uncanny to some. But to me, it was just what I needed to shift my total identity on motherhood. It was not about 'doing' parenthood properly. The gift, I believe, is about being myself and respecting others to be themselves. We both grow through the learning partnership. So the gift surfaces from my unconscious.

The success

Jett was born healthy. My blood pressure dropped to normal pretty soon after.

Was it a fluke? Whether it was using the Force to bomb the Death Star, or listening to the wisdom of my inner self to get past death by blood pressure, the supreme ordeal is a one-off event. Thankfully.

So what is the use of the gift, if you can only use it once?

The call to return

From the learnings in the inner supernatural world, the 'call to return' from abstract intuition to the real world beckons. How can I consciously use the gift over and over to reap the ultimate reward on a day-to-day basis?

Acceptance: transition back to physical outer world from the intuitive inner world

Luke Skywalker returns with a new identity of a warrior. He is forever changed when he gets back to the real world. No longer is he a farmer. He is now a Jedi, ready to overthrow the Dark Side.

I have intellectualised the concepts of joyful parenthood, and how being true to myself will ultimately inspire others to achieve their highest purpose. Certainly I have come through with new beliefs, values and identity on parenthood. I am now ready to be a role model of how to overcome anxiety and apprehension to live our dreams. I shall foster learning partnerships from one another. Walk my talk: I will help other parents find joy in their own lives, live it well, love life and leave a legacy to their children to do the same.

The reward

What is the ultimate 'reward'? It is about using the gift as a strength in your life. To do your calling? To be true to thyself? The hero's journey then spirals to the next level – as a new call to adventure begins.

Luke Skywalker battles the dark side as his next call to adventure. Yours truly finds it rewarding to hang up the dentist's drill and become a facilitator of leadership transformation in order to unleash self-actualisation at organisational as well as individual level.

Are you now perceiving yourself as your greatest hero? Or do you see it all as the agony of a lifelong quest? After all, nobody can live your life for you. How will you answer the call to adventure and experience the revelation of the mysteries in your life.

It is all up to you, playpals. Choose to lose your mind, and come to your senses. Become aware of your hero's journey. Accept the call, and begin the adventure. *Avatar*, anyone?

Some final musings

We have been doing a lot of *think*ing about how to 'lose our minds' and 'come to our senses'. In short, what it is like to be a playpal. To wrap up, reflect on what other things you can choose to *do* or not in order to *get* the results you want for you, your family, your work tribe, your greater community, your world. Remember: being a playpal is meant to be joyful – although it may take some effort – because the task will not seem as heavy when the spirit is light.

I started the discussion with looking at the most basic unit of the tribe: the family. Let's go back and review other contexts in your life.

Personal learning journal

What would you *stop*?

What would you *continue*?

What would you *start*?

List at least one key insight.

1.

Parenting can be hard – especially if you have been finding it challenging to 'read the book' that is your child. It takes intention, attention and action – planning, persistence and practice, practice, practice.

So, what does it mean for *you* to be a parent? What is *your* intention as a parent? How will you fulfil this? What do you commit to do? What is your first step?

What it means to be a parent for me

Parenting is about loving unconditionally, leading a great life, and leaving a legacy: inspiring my children to do the same – to love life and lead a great life according to them.

My intention is to be a playpal – a *p*ractising *l*eader *a*vidly *y*earning *p*artnerships *at* *l*earning: I simply love the perspectives that I learn from my children and those I meet on my parenting journey, and what I pass on along the way.

I commit to living my pass-I-on, and leaving the planet better than I found it – every day and in every way.

My first step is to 'pass-I-on' at least once every twenty-four hours.

Remember that saying 'the hand that rocks the cradle rules the world'? Start kidding yourself. Kids rule. Parent leadership rocks!

Acknowledgements

There are many people who contributed in various ways to this book, and I am most grateful for them.

First, I would like to thank Lynora Brooke, meditation coach and friend, who put me in touch with David Martin from Allen & Unwin – they both encouraged me to pen this book. Through David I met Jan Roberts, bestselling author of the four-book 'Better Babies' series, who initially thought we could collaborate on a parenting book that would make the fifth in her series. Upon the completion of my contribution, Jan felt it could stand alone as a book, and we started looking at publishers to get it birthed into the world. Thank you, Jan, for writing the foreword to *Intentional Parenting*.

There have been others who have encouraged me on this journey, and I would like to acknowledge their contribution:

Dr Stephanie Burns, Learning to Learn expert and mentor, inspired me towards rejuvenating my love of facilitating learning twenty years ago, and she has now become an inspiration to my own children. Glenn Doman, whose work with brain-injured children at The Institutes for the Achievement of Human Potential ignited my interest and curiosity in The Gentle Revolution and evolving the joy of learning. Philippa Bond – friend, colleague, mentor and training creator extraordinaire – supported and challenged me over ten years to be the best I can be in my area of passion. She was courageous to put me in front of her workshops to share my early, crude version of 'Parent Leadership' to her delegates. Angela Chia, entrepreneur, primary school best friend, one of my first playpals – her unwavering belief in an old friend's passion for the Parent Leadership message put her own reputation on the line to raise funds to actualise three years' worth of keynote engagements and workshops on parenting and leadership in the Malaysian Government Civil Service, Ministry of Education, Family and Welfare and women's groups. Victoria Yuille-Furey, fellow meta-coach, parent and staunch playpal, showed faith in this work and tried the 'principles of learning partnership' in parenting with her two beautiful girls, Zimena and Aurelia. Colin James, advanced communications speaker, teacher and mentor, whose belief in me over the years has accelerated this book into being. Dr Michael Hall, Neuro-Semantics founder, trainer, author and friend, who encouraged leadership in fields of our passion and for us to express it accordingly. Michelle Duval, Meta-Coach Training System co-founder, author and friend, who coached me to unleash this Parent Leadership pioneering spirit in me. Rodney Marks, past president of the National Speakers Association of Australia, comedian and mentor, who focused my energies to hone my Parent Leadership message. Susie Cameron, *Small Fry* co-author, communications expert and fellow playpal, inspired the delivery of this book to leave a legacy with ease and grace. Rosina Mladenovic, fellow Meta-Coach, author and playpal, who constantly provided loving feedback to the project and the crafting of the Seven Rs framework. Paul Sparks, Sales Effectiveness expert, colleague and editor of my contribution to the first volume of his *Sales Compendium*. His appreciation of my writing style pushed me over the edge to accelerate the publication of this book. Michelle Richmond, sustainability coach, energy expert and playpal, whose encouragement and assistance in aligning my intentions and dissolving my inner fears helped to be the midwife and fairy godmother in the delivery of this book.

Paul Mitchell, leadership facilitator and principal of The Human Enterprise, whose generosity of spirit inspired the title of the book.

Thanks also to Jennifer Beck, Robin Elliot, Rod Power,

ACKNOWLEDGEMENTS

Debra Wilde, Graham Richardson, Cheryl Gilroy, Suzy Jacobs, Billy Kirkley, Corinne Cantor, Rich Hirst, whose words of encouragement continue to echo in my ears and propel me to actualise this project . . . and to countless others whose lives have touched mine and who have contributed to a learning partnership – whether they were aware of it or not.

Last but not least are my constant learning partners and closest playpals: Ken Ho, my lowng-suffering husband and co-parent in our tribe, the two brilliant mirrors that are my beautiful children, Jett and Xian. Love and appreciation, of course, to my parents, Jerry and Alice Sum, who started it all with their own tribe, consisting of my gorgeous sisters, Elaine, Eydie and Eleanor, and their extended tribes.

To those who have picked up *Intentional Parenting*, I would love to hear from you about your leadership lessons and how you are practising as a leader. Please drop me a line to share them so that I may begin a yet-unexplored learning partnership with you.

Dr Yvonne Sum
www.dryvonnesum.com

Please contact my office for speaking engagements and personal coaching on +61 2 8014 8858.

Just curious and want to interact with me about my work? Connect with me on:
http://www.dryvonnesum.com/blog/
http://www.youtube.com/user/dryvonnesum
http://www.linkedin.com/in/dryvonnesum
http://www.facebook.com/ParentAsLeader
http://www.facebook.com/DrYvonneSum
https://twitter.com/YvonneSum

Bibliography

Bond, Philippa. *Coaching Wisdom*, Inform Training & Research, 2002.

Bond, Philippa. *NLP Practitioner and Master Practitioner Manual*, Inform Training & Research, 2002.

Bandler, Richard and Grinder, John. *Patterns of the Hypnotic Techniques of Milton H. Erickson, M.D.* vol. 1, Meta Publications, Cupertino, CA, 1975.

Bandler, Richard and Grinder, John. *Reframing: Neuro-Linguistic Programming and the Transformation of Meaning*, Real Bandler. Bandler, Richard and Grinder, John. *The Structure of Magic*. Science and Behaviour Books, CA, 1975.

Buzan, Tony. *The Power of Spiritual Intelligence*, Thorsons, London, 2001.

Caliper report. *The Qualities that Distinguish Women Leaders*, 2005.

Cialdini, Robert. *Influence: The New Psychology of Modern Persuasion*, Quill, NY, 1984.

Covey, Stephen M.R., *The Speed of Trust*, Free Press, New York, 2006.

Czikszentmihalyi, Mihalyi. *Flow: The Psychology of Optimal Experience*, Harper & Row, NY, 1991.

Dilts, Robert B. *Strategies of Genius*, vol. 1, Meta Publications, 1994.

Dilts, Robert B.;Hallbom, Tim and Smith, Suzi. *Beliefs: Pathways to Health and Wellbeing*, Metamorphous Press, Portland, 1991.

Doman, Glen. *How to Teach Your Baby to Read*, Better Baby Press, 1990.

Drucker, Peter F. *Management Challenges for the 21st Century*, HarperBusiness, NY, 1999.

Ellis, Albert and Harper, Robert A. *A Guide to Rational Living*, Wilshire Book Co., Chatsworth, CA, 1969.

Epictetus. *The Discourses: Books 1–4*, NuVision Publications, Sioux Falls, SD, 2006.

Gardner, Howard. *Intelligence Reframed: Multiple Intelligences for the 21st Century*, Basic Books, New York, 1999.

Gladwell, Malcolm. *Blink*, Back Bay Books, NY, 2005.

Gladwell, Malcolm. *The Tipping Point*, Abacus, UK, 2000.

Gladwell, Malcolm. *Outliers*, Back Bay Books, NY, 2008.

Godin, Seth. *Tribes*, Penguin Books, NY, 2008.

Goffee, Rob and Jones, Gareth. *Why Should Anyone Be Led By You?*, Harvard Business School Press, 2006.

Goleman, Daniel. *Emotional Intelligence: Why It Can Matter More Than IQ*, Bloomsbury, UK, 1996.

Goleman, Daniel; Boyatzis, Richard and McKee, Annie. *Primal Leadership*, Harvard Business School Press, USA, 2002.

Graves, Clare W. 'Human Nature Prepares for a Momentous Leap', *The Futurist*, April, 1974.

Hall. L.M. and Duval, M. *Meta-Coaching Vol. 1: Coaching Change*, Neuro-Semantics Publications, USA, 2004.

Hall. L.M. *Unleashing Leadership in Self-Actualizing Organizations*, Neuro-Semantics Publications, USA, 2009.

Hewlett, S.; Sherbin, L. and Sumberg, K. 'How Gen Y and Baby Boomers Will Reshape Your Agenda', Harvard Business Review, July, 2009.

Hunsaker, P. and Alessandra, A. *The Art of Managing People*, Simon & Schuster, NY, 1980.

Laborde, Genie. *Fine Tune Your Brain*, Syntony Publishing, CA, 1988.

Laborde, Genie. *Influencing with Integrity: Management Skills for Communication and Negotiation*, Syntony Publishing, CA, 1987.

Loehr, Jim and Schwartz, Tony. *The Power of Full Engagement*, Allen & Unwin, Australia, 2003.

Maxwell, John C. *The 21 Irrefutable Laws of Leadership*, Thomas Nelson, USA, 2007.

McCarthy, Bernice. *The 4MAT System: Teaching to Learning Styles with Right/Left Mode Techniques*, Excel Publishing Inc., Barrington, IL, 1980, 1987.

Myers, Isabel B. with Peter B. *Gifts Differing: Understanding*

Personality Type, Davies-Black Publishing, Palo Alto, CA, 1995.

Meares, Ainslie. *The Hidden Powers of Leadership*, Hill of Content, Melbourne, Australia, 1978.

Neville, Bernie. *Educating Psyche: Emotion, Imagination and the Unconscious in Learning*, Collins Dove, 1989.

O'Connor, J. and Seymour, J. *Training with NLP: Skills for Managers, Trainers and Communicators*, Thorsons, London, UK, 1994.

O'Reilly, Charles A. III and Pfeffer, Jeffrey. *Hidden Value*, Harvard Business School Press, Boston, 2000.

University of Pennsylvania Positive Psych Center, The Penn Resiliency Project, 2007.

Seligman, Martin. *Authentic Happiness*, Random House Australia, 2002.

Semler, Ricardo. *The Seven-Day Weekend*, Random House, London, 2003.

Sum, Yvonne. 'Doing It Right', *Dental Asia*, November, 2005.

Sum, Yvonne. 'The 7Rs of Parenting', eCourse online, 2007.

Sum, Yvonne. 'The Magic of Rapport', *Dental Asia*, September, 2002.

Sum, Yvonne. 'The Magic of Suggestive Language', *Dental Asia*, March, 2003.

Sum, Yvonne, 'The Magic of Wisdom Training', *Dental Asia*, June, 2003.

Sum, Yvonne. 'Simple Joys of Parenthood', *Dental Asia*, July, 2005.

Sum, Yvonne. 'Relationship Intelligence: How You Are Managing Change?' *Dental Asia*, May, 2004.

Suzuki, Shinichi. *Nurtured by Love*, Warner Brothers Publications, USA, 2nd Edition, 1983.

Thunder Strikes with Jan Orsi. *Song of the Deer: The Great Sun Dance Journey of the Soul*, Jaguar Books. Malibu, CA. 1999.

Warby, Sheila. *With Love in My Heart and a Twinkle in My Ear: A Parent's Guide to Suzuki Education*, Suzuki Talent Education Association of Australia, NSW, 3rd Edition, 2002.

Woodsmall, W. and James, T. *Time Line and the Basis of Personality*, Meta Publications, USA, 1988.